Nicaragua 1984

Reagan's Forgotten War

Rachael L. Lehmberg

ISBN: 1460936760
ISBN-13: 9781460936764

Dedication

This book is dedicated to my wonderful, supportive family: my husband and best friend, David, for his endless patience and encouragement, my sons for literary suggestions and computer help, and to the people of Nicaragua, especially the children.

Table of Contents

Preface   vii

Chapter 1   *Holy Week*   *1*

Chapter 2   *Away From Home Alone*   *19*

Chapter 3   *First Impressions of Managua*   *29*

Chapter 4   *We Explore the Countryside
             and Attend a Campesino Mass*   *37*

Chapter 5   *The Press*   *53*

Chapter 6   *The Miskitu Indian Question*   *71*

Chapter 7   *From Catholic to Protestant
             and Back Again*   *81*

Chapter 8   *Elections and Health Care*   *107*

Chapter 9   *Reforestation and Human Rights*   *123*

Chapter 10   *From the U.S. Embassy to Corinto*   *135*

Chapter 11 *We Meet a Commandante*
and Salvadoran Refugees *145*

Chapter 12 *Into the War Zone* *155*

Chapter 13 *The Ocotal Women's Group* *181*

Chapter 14 *Home Again* *189*

Afterword **193**

Preface – 2011

In our local bookstore, part of a nationwide chain, there is a table bearing the sign "Reagan Centennial." More than a dozen hardback books lie, face up, on this table. They all have pretty much the same cover – a picture of a grandfatherly Ronald Reagan wearing his trademark crooked, yet courageous, grin. As I walked past this table last night, a single object caught my eye: it was a small paperback book lying on top of one of the hardback ones. The book was entitled, *The Great Tragedies of Shakespeare.* The cover bore the subtitles, *Macbeth, King Lear, Hamlet, and Othello.* I smiled at what I took to be a silent, sardonic comment by some unknown dissenter during this "honor Reagan" year.

But when I passed by the table again a few minutes later, Shakespeare had been whisked away – a casualty perhaps of what has become today's political correctness – a kind of presidential sainthood for Ronald Wilson Reagan.

It occurred to me that now, almost thirty years past Reagan's presidency, a whole generation has grown up. It's a generation to whom the word *"Contra"* means little, and *"Sandinista,"* even less. In Nicaragua, the children I visited (at least the ones who lived) have grown up also.

So why have I exhumed my journal, with its dusty, yellowed pages from the bottom drawer of my desk?

Iran-Contra, if it's mentioned at all in most Reagan biographies, is seen as a small blip in the great man's "legacy" - just a moment of inattention in the schedule of an otherwise ever-watchful Chief Executive. Now, when I do a computer search for "*Contra*," up pops a link to a video game. But to the people of Nicaragua in 1984, the name, "*Contra*" was no game. It denoted a constant and terrifying threat; a sound of gunfire in the night that brought torture and death to non-combatant men, women, and children. Ronald Reagan called the Contra force, "Freedom Fighters."

Yet, far from being a gallant counter revolutionary army, Contra forces consisted mostly of remnants of the deposed dictator, Somoza's personal guardsmen and friends along with mercenaries and a few Miskitu Indians who were too confused and isolated to know whom to trust. Arms purchased by proceeds from the illegal sales of weapons to Iran, were sent to them, with or without the knowledge of then-president Ronald Reagan, who maintained "plausible deniability" either by his own decision or the decisions of his advisors.

The names and faces of some of those advisors are familiar: Gates, Negroponte, Abrams, and others. One figure in particular has recently held unprecedented power. In 1986, he was a representative from Wyoming and ranking Republican on a House select committee charged with investigating the Iran-Contra affair. In his Minority Report, he insisted that the real scandal was not that President Reagan secretly sold arms to Iran to finance the Contra War after Congress had cut off the funds for the Contra, but that Congress had overstepped its authority by interfering with the President's foreign policy powers. That representative's name was Dick Cheney.

Like the powerful figures in Shakespeare's plays, these men have brought tragedy, but not on themselves, on the people of Nicaragua.

* * *

I have changed the names of the people who traveled with me to protect their privacy, but the names of our interviewees in Nicaragua have not been changed as their intention was to be quoted "on the record."

Rachael Lehmberg
2011

Honduras

PuertoCabezas

Atlantic

Ocotal

Nicaragua

Esteli

Matagalpa

Corinto

Leon

Masaya

Managua ★ Granada

Bluefields

Lake Nicaragua

Pacific

San Juan del Norte

Costa Rica

ⓒ Rachael Lehmberg 2011

Ocotal

Chapter One

Holy Week

April 18, 1984

In the dream last night, I am performing an act that is semi-automatic for me, an average Southern Californian. I am driving my car along a freeway. It is a nameless freeway and my destination is vague. All I know was that I am heading north and that I am taking a carload of children somewhere where they were about to enjoy the day: to the beach or maybe to Disneyland.

When I glance into my rearview mirror, preliminary to changing lanes, I see that a terrible accident is occurring behind me. Cars and trucks are careening into each other, falling in twisted heaps off the overpass. I know that I should be horrified but my reactions are oddly blunted. It is clear that people are dead and injured, but it seemed to have nothing to do with us. My responsibility is for my own passengers, my children (magically young again) and their friends. The proper authorities will take care of the freeway carnage. All I want is to get safely away.

I say to myself, *"Keep going. Don't upset the children."*

But a strange thing happens. Instead of feeling relieved by my decision, I feel worse. The farther north I drive, the more my anxiety increases until at last, as we cross the Oregon border, I am shaking violently with fear and cold. I had made the wrong choice and I knew it. It is the shaking that wakes me. The dream association with Oregon is clear as soon as I identify the dripping sound outside–rain. The cold is easy, too. Our treacherous California spring has slipped away in the night leaving a gust of cold air to flutter the drapes in front of the open bedroom window.

Remembering that the dogs are outside in the rain, I grope for my bathrobe and slip out of bed, being careful as I do so not to disturb Dave. I can't see him in the dark but I know he is there, lying curled on one side with the bridge of his nose pinched between his thumb and forefinger. He always sleeps that way as if he unconsciously misses the pressure of his eyeglasses on the bridge of his nose. I don't turn on the light. He needs his sleep. Easter is just days away and when I think of how many of our minister friends had their heart attacks at Easter or Christmas… well, I just try to be a little more careful.

I pad barefoot through the dark house past the gray mounds that I know as furniture. As soon as I open the garage door for the dogs, they run inside shaking themselves, grateful that someone had finally remembered to rescue them. I dash back to the warmth and safety of bed, still shaking despite my bathrobe.

It is only when I insinuate myself against the curves of Dave's sleeping body that my shaking begins to ease and now I am able to give the fear a name. I have finally made the decision that I've been fretting over for two weeks–I have decided to go to Nicaragua.

In isn't until the dream that I have any conception of the size of the fear that I have been gestating since the phone call last week. Now it has been brought kicking and screaming into consciousness and I see, only too clearly, that there is no room for it in my life. When the lady from the ecumenical agency called me from San Francisco and asked if I wanted to be part of a fact finding team going to Nicaragua in May, I should have just said "no thanks," and hung up. After all, Nicaragua has already been thoroughly combed by experts. What facts can I, an ordinary schoolteacher and housewife, find that the experts have managed to overlook? Maybe some crumbs of fact had been swept off into a corner where I, with my practiced housewife's eye, will see them? Now <u>really</u>! Why don't I just admit I was flattered that someone would call me long distance with an important sounding invitation? I will call her back, thank her for the complement and tell her to find an expert to go in my place.

And then there is the cost – nine hundred dollars. Wouldn't it be more responsible to donate the money, if indeed we could raise it at all, to some church relief agency? Or, I ask myself coldly, is the cost of the trip just an easy excuse not to go? Cowardice masquerading as penury.

Why should I get involved in the problems of Latin America anyway? What is it to me? If I'm honest, I have to admit that my life is richer and more comfortable because of the exploitation of the Third World. I like bananas as well as the next person and they are usually cheaper than the oranges that are grown in the grove down the road. No mystery about why imported fruit should be cheaper than domestic: the workers in Central America are paid less than American workers, it's as simple as that.

Now, I do love my summer cottons - white and crisp to show off my beach tan. Why should I care that Central American children pick that cotton for 25 cents a day? As long as prices stay low enough, I can fill my closet. So what if peasant farmers were forced off the land by the thousands during the cotton boom of the last twenty years? What's it to me?

I benefit from poverty in other ways, too. My teacher's annuity funds are invested in multinational corporations that have assembly plants in so called "developing countries." Do you think I want to pay those workers more if it means less profit for me? Heck no. Let 'em eat bananas. Except...

I am standing again on the wharf in a hell-hole of a town on the northern coast of Peru. The year is 1979 and Dave and I are the leaders of a group of Methodist college students. We had been sent to study "the Latin American Reality."

We are surrounded by a stinking haze tinted pinkish-yellow by the setting sun. The smell is the only part of the day's catch that remains in Peru. Cargo ships are moving slowly out to sea, floating like bloated carcasses, bellies filled with fishmeal to feed cattle that will someday be Quarter Pounders and Super Tacos. Peru has a huge national debt and to help pay it, the fish meal plant was sold to a North American fast food chain. "Have it your way." Don't we always? And why does Peru have that debt? It's partly as a result of the Trojan Horse generosity of the American people. Our government thinks Peru needs weapons, lots of weapons. In fact, a few days before I had been looking up the barrel of one of them, a machine gun, on the streets of Lima. My crime? Being in the vicinity of a street demonstration. The demonstration was in support of a general strike by people who didn't understand why they couldn't have enough to eat in a land that exports more than it consumes. I don't blame them. I can't understand it either, but the American people have ordained that weapons of internal repression are more important than the food that would make those weapons unnecessary.

Our study tour began in June 1979, the same month that television brought the agony of the Nicaraguan revolution into everyone's living room. As our plane soared 30,000 feet above Central America, we watched "California Suite" on the movie screen. From time to time, I pulled aside the window shade and looked out into the dark wondering why the unreal movie seemed more real and immediate to me than the fact that people were killing and dying down there.

We observed the progress of the Nicaraguan Revolution from the south rather than, like most Americans, from the north down. I don't know if that made any difference to us in practical terms, but when you hear about Somoza, the U.S. supported dictator of Nicaragua, bombing his own cities, then the next day you are routinely tear gassed just for being in the proverbial "wrong place at the wrong time," you understand, *truly* understand, that in Latin America there are no innocent bystanders.

We spent that summer of 1979 living in an old house in downtown Lima, hearing lectures from theologians and missionaries, and taking trips in crowded, worn out buses or the trains that see-sawed their way across the Andes. Much of that time is lost to me now, faded into a haze of grayness and constant gastroenteritis, but certain moments remain with the clarity of still photos: A toddler playing with an empty milk can in the shade of the stiffened body of a dead dog; "Blowing in the Wind," sung in Spanish, drifting out of the door of a tiny church on Sunday morning; children waiting patiently for us to finish eating our dinner so they could have the leftovers from our plates; the sound of *"El Condor Pasa"* played on a reed flute floating out over the consummate cold of an Andean night; and men, women and children clamoring over the seats of the emptying excursion train from Machu Picchu to grab the rotting remains of the tourists' box lunches.

Nineteen seventy-nine was the summer of Skylab. In a thin international Edition of *Time* that somebody bought on one of our infrequent sorties inside the Lima Sheraton, (it was a handy place to buy stamps) we discovered that the satellite with the decaying orbit was being treated as something of a campy joke in the U.S. We saw pictures of tee shirts and hats suitably inscribed for the occasion and read about the parties that would be held on the night that the dead hunk of metal was expected to fall. For the South Americans, however, Skylab was no joke. They knew, as did the folks who were planning the parties, that it wouldn't fall on the United States. To them it seemed no quirk of chance that our garbage would come to rest somewhere in the Southern Hemisphere. They were used to receiving our cast-offs and usually they ended up paying for them, too.

For me as a North American that summer in Peru was a painful shock, a bit like catching a glimpse of myself obliquely in a store window and discovering that I was no longer as young or as thin as I had hoped.

I used to feel very smug about being a citizen of the United States. My father was an immigrant from Hungary. As a child during World War II, I was always conscious that, but for a quirk of Fate and a short boat ride, I would be among the suffering children of Europe. But more than that, I was proud that I lived in a country whose soldiers gave candy bars to children instead of running them through with bayonets.

We had been back from Peru only a few months when I turned on the radio one day as a newscaster was saying, "...border patrolmen today completed recovery of the bodies of the thirteen Salvadorans who died in the desert while attempting to enter the United States illegally."

So there it was, what we knew had to happen sooner or later: the troubles of Latin America on our own doorstep. What could be so terrible in El Salvador that people were willing to risk the desert in summer to escape? I knew the answer because I had glimpsed it in a small way in Peru. It was the wrath of the rich and privileged class who accused anyone who didn't quietly accept grinding poverty of being a "Communist" and therefore a legitimate target for torture and death. Our own government had only to hear the words "Communist Threat" and a stream of money flowed forth. It was the weapons purchased with that money that were driving the Salvadorans from their homes and into my life.

That was when I began working with church groups who were lobbying for refugee status for Salvadorans and that was how the lady in San Francisco got my name. But how can I go to Nicaragua when I am already emotionally overextended with the Salvadoran problem? I can't take any more frustration. I wish they would send some expert instead of me.

April 19 (Maundy Thursday)

Dave took me out to lunch this noon. We went to one of our favorite spots, the Pomona Valley Mining Company. The restaurant, which is supposed to look like a derelict mining shaft, is perched on top of a hill. Funny thing, if it really were an old building, the city would probably insist on having it torn down as an eyesore, but since it only looks as if it were old, it's okay.

Dave was absorbed in the process of mentally composing his Easter sermon, so I just gazed out the window. A lush, lavish view was spread before me. Trees and houses filled the valley with the homey perfection of model railroad scenery. The freeway flowed directly beneath us and beyond that, the pale buildings of a defense plant snuggled against the green heart of the

Pomona Valley. All around us our fellow diners grazed peacefully on salads as we watched fat clouds roll by. Conversations hummed around us and occasionally I caught fragments out of context.

The two men at the table in front of us seemed to be salesmen. The one in the green plaid sport coat was saying to the one whose back was turned to me, "now every guy who goes out and buys a home wants a radial saw, right? For whatever dumb, American reason, he *wants a radial saw.*"

I couldn't hear the reply.

A cocktail waitress, dressed appropriate to the decor in abbreviated miner's coveralls, seemed to be making a lot of stops at the table on the other side of us. Because the table was behind me, I couldn't see the occupants, but the decibel level of their disembodied voices grew steadily until the conversation began to chew on my eardrums.

"I hear that weapon can fire 2800 rounds..."

"Oh, the weapon is capable of 6,000 rounds, but in short bursts. Keep that going long and you'll melt the barrel."

"So what do you do if you've got multiple threats?"

"Well you gotta saturate the field. See, the problem is that the barrel will shut down and..."

"Saturate the field." That means people, I think. People just like the ones living in those Dick and Jane houses down there. That means metal tearing through flesh. That means somebody's son or daughter who learned to toddle and then to run, maybe to dance, a process taking years, is blotted out in an instant. I turned completely around in my chair wondering as I did so, what kind of monsters I would confront.

But they were just three pleasant young men, one of them rather handsome with a neatly trimmed beard. They all wore nice suits and no doubt, their mothers are quite proud of them.

Today is Maundy Thursday. At the service tonight I heard the Good Friday story as I do every year and, as always the horror is blunted by familiarity. But one sentence thrust itself out of the children's sermon and attached itself to me as if I had never heard it before: "Jesus was nailed to a cross so that he would die." Perhaps I never heard it stated quite that way before, or perhaps I not quite listened before. Wasn't it usually "Jesus was nailed to a cross <u>and</u> he died?" Interesting how one simple syntactical change, the substitution of a subordinator for a coordinator, should make such a difference. The matter of intent, I suppose, the difference between first and second-degree murder. Did the three gentlemen in the restaurant understand this? Do they understand the affront against God contained in the act of taking a perfectly functioning, healthy body and deliberately making it die?

At the close of the service, the ritual stripping of the sanctuary began. Of all of the ceremonies of the church year, that is the one I find most moving. As the organ played "Were You There When They Crucified My Lord," Dave and the choir members removed the candles, the altar cloth, the banners: all the familiar accessories of the chancel. Finally, after the choir had filed out, the lights dimmed and went out, too. We were left, all of us, standing in darkness. The sanctuary began to feel like a tomb with the large window behind the altar as its only opening. Far away, on a mountaintop, two little lights glowed. Standing there in the darkness with all the other silent, hidden bodies close around me; I felt the weight of all of their struggles and pain, which I know something about after four years in the parsonage here. I felt flooded, as I often do, with a wordless love for these people. They try so hard and mean well, most of them. But I can't help wondering; how will they feel when they hear that I'm going to a country of which our President so vehemently disapproves?

Saturday, April 21

Good Friday (yesterday) passed in a blur. I thought it would have some great significance for me this year, but I missed it in a flurry of behind the scenes tasks. It was our turn to have the traditional three hour community service at our church so I found myself running here and there trying to get preachers and liturgists to the right spots at the right times with the right books. Except for one lost robe and some minor confusions, things went pretty well and afterwards Dave and I went to the movies. It was a communion and benediction to sit in the popcorn smelly darkness, hold hands and laugh.

This morning is overpoweringly brilliant, the kind of morning you have in Southern California after a storm has swept away all the old smog and the new smog hasn't had time to insinuate itself yet. Dave and I are having breakfast at Square One, sitting at the little white tables outdoors under sunlight pre-strained through green *Cinzano* umbrellas. He is reading the Times and I am writing in my notebook.   Tubbed flowers and varying degrees of greenness surrounded us. I could spend the rest of my life having breakfast at Square One and lunch at Walter's. Or the other way around once in awhile–for variety. All that is really expected of me is that I show up on Sunday mornings and smile. Actually, that's probably what some church members would prefer over my present course of action.

"David," I say tentatively. He is reading the sports section and I hate to bother him.

"Humm?"

"When Jesus said, 'let this cup pass from me,' do you think he was thinking about dying or about the alienation from his friends?"

He looks a bit surprised. "Well, I don't know. I guess what you' re asking is which is worse, physical or emotional suffering, aren't you?"

I chew my thumbnail reflectively. "I guess I am."

"Well, I can only answer for myself, I suppose, but it seems to me that in my life I've felt more fear of emotional pain than of physical pain."

"Yeah, me too."

Afternoon

Dave officiates at a society wedding and comes home with his honorarium–a hundred dollar bill that he drops casually in my lap. "For your trip," he says. His hand cups my shoulder.

Tuesday, April 24

Easter was, like Good Friday, too big and public to leave room for much spiritual focus for me. I sat through two of the three services preoccupied with the responses of the other worshippers. Many of them were total strangers to me and I wanted to be sure that they knew what they'd been missing all year. Did they like the music? Were they happy with the sermon? There were the usual whisperings–agreement with a point or *sub rosa* criticisms. Actually, that's why I always sit in the back of the church. To paraphrase the Big Bad Wolf, "the better to see you, m'dear." From behind, it's easier to judge reactions in the almost imperceptible nodding and shaking of heads, the knowing or I-told-you-so looks between husband and wife. And the backs, well…. faces can lie even when they don't intend to, but backs, being mute, cannot. Shoulders tell stories that faces would deny.

We are driving home now from a few days rest in San Diego where our son, Randy and his wife are college students. They are excited about my trip and anxious to hear about what I will learn. My son said, "I've had too many roommates to believe in socialism." I understand what he's saying and it's an important point to investigate. How does Nicaragua, or any socialist country deal with Roommate Syndrome? China,

Cuba, and Nicaragua have all been heavily criticized for their neighborhood committees, often characterized as "snoopers," yet social pressure seems to be the best way to deal with Roommate Syndrome. After all, which is kinder, to characterize a whole class of people as "welfare chiselers" and cut their allowances for food and medical care, or to deal with the human proclivity towards sloth on a case by case basis?

We stayed too long at the beach and now, in order for Dave to make it back for an evening meeting, we find ourselves locked in rush hour freeway traffic. The day is hot. Pale yellow smog clings to the horizon like bathtub scum.

The radio sends a steady stream of traffic advice, but still we crawl along. "There's an injury accident on the Santa Monica this afternoon. A paramedic call has gone out so avoid the Santa Monica west of Normandy and now here is Donna Dower who has just escaped from Orange County, Donna?"

"Yes, Bill, things are looking bad down in Orange County. It's stop and go on the Santa Ana all the way to San Clemente. The swallows may be back in Capistrano, but they got there by air folks! And that's all from KFI in the Sky."

A trailer truck loaded with flattened cardboard boxes looms next to us. A blond, curly haired young woman slides her elongated pick up truck on our other side. The truck is grandly decorated with flames and the words "Hellcat Racers." Her elbow sticks out of the open window and her radio blares some kind of deep, throbbing music.

Dave is getting cross and tired, but he is restrained as always and simply says, "why is it that people who like music like that always think everyone else does, too?"

I change the station on the radio. "There's another injury accident slowing things down this afternoon..." I click the radio off and address Dave's profile. "Does it ever seem to you that human suffering ought to be treated with a little more respect?"

"Well, I'd prefer some other music, but I'd hardly characterize what I'm doing as suffering."

"I'm sorry! I didn't mean the music," I said, giving his thigh a friendly squeeze, "I meant the traffic reports. They always sound like injured people are just obstructions, just getting in the way of the rest of us who are in such a hurry to go home to our own safe little worlds."

"Yes, well, it's pretty tough to report tragedy with sensitivity especially in that context."

"Yeah, I know. Maybe it's necessary for us to be a little bit numb. There's just too much pain around to take it all seriously."

Rows of new townhouses, each thrusting a garage out in front of it like a hostage, squat in a dusty field. I try to imagine all the families that live in them, try to see them as individuals. I can't do it. All I can grasp is a vague sense of a sea of humanity all wanting to make their parents proud of them by being successful–wanting to be good children which has somehow gotten confused with buying the right things and "moving up," always moving, moving fast. Was that why we started getting mean-spirited as a nation when the Arabs slowed us down by raising the price of oil? Freedom seems to be the same as motion to us – physical mobility in our gas tanks and social mobility in our bank accounts.

In front of us is a pink Cadillac with two bumper stickers. One says "I [heart] Jesus" and the other, I guess, is supposed to say, "Tough Times Never Last But Tough People Do." A crack in the bumper has swallowed the middle line of the sticker, though, so the message reads, "Tough Times Never...People Do." I like that better than the original. I have begun to feel very sad about the way the word "Tough" is applied to people and to policies. Why do we worship that quality so? Have we given up on tenderness?

Monday, April 30

Being tough and winning, those are the two things that Americans seem preoccupied with right now. Dave and I are at Sneakers having a beer after our evening meetings. Sneakers is a kind of temple to the cult of The Winner. Photos of baseball stars cover the walls. Between and above the photos, giant Day-Glo figures performing every imaginable sport are painted on the walls. A huge inflatable beer can hangs over the bar and just below it; an electronic scoreboard rolls a continuous stream of baseball scores. A giant TV screen commands one corner while smaller screens are set, like side altars in a cathedral, in niches around the room. Waiters and waitresses, dressed in athletic clothes, jog between the tables looking, except for their trays and aprons, as if they had just wandered in off the courts.

Dave is watching a baseball game that seems to have taken place at some unspecified time in the past. I have fallen into a vague funk. I'm already feeling alienated from my environment and I haven't even gone anywhere yet.

The congregation has been wonderful about my trip, I've even received unsolicited donations for some of my expenses, but I feel increasingly unequal to the responsibility of Finding Facts. Will I know them when I see them? What if my Facts conflict with the government's Facts? Why should people believe me? And why am I opening myself to the pain of controversy? I'm hurting from it already. Saturday, Dave's mother called while I was at the grocery store and asked Dave why I was going to "that Communist country." She made it clear to him that she's worried I will damage his career. What if she's right?

Certainly if there is a confrontation between Nicaragua and the U.S. there is no doubt that the present government of Nicaragua will come out the loser. And why should I want to be on the side of a loser? Losers are the lepers of the Eighties.

Dave reaches across the table and takes my hand. "How was your shopping trip with Jeanne, today," he asks.

"Oh fine. We had a good time."

"Where did you go?"

"Just over to the Mall. She helped me pick out a skirt and some pants for the trip. My only other summer ones are tan and I can't wear those..."

"Why not?"

"It was in that letter they sent me, they said don't wear anything khaki– that means tan."

"No? Why not?" His face was instantly alert.

"Well...you know...so no one will get mixed up and accidentally...you know...mistake me for a soldier."

"You're not going anywhere near the fighting are you?"

"Well...there is a part of the itinerary that...well... how can a person Find Facts if she doesn't go to the war zone?"

"Can't you just skip that part of the trip?"

"I don't know, maybe. I'll have to see what happens."

"Well, try," he says firmly and turns back to the base-ball game.

Chapter Two

Away From Home Alone

May 19

Here I am at one in the morning flying away from friends and family at something like 500 miles an hour. It is not hot in the plane, but sweat beads my upper lip. Maybe I'm going to faint. Every hour puts another 500 miles between me and all that I know, all that I am. With every hour, Dave is five hundred miles further away from me. Leaving him back at the airport was like an amputation. I must be crazy. Just what do I think I am going to accomplish?

I keep hearing the voice of our daughter, who took me aside on the night of our son's graduation from college two weeks ago. In my mind I hear her over and over telling me "it would kill Dad if anything happened to you." Certainly I don't think I'm in any more danger in Nicaragua than I would be driving on the San Bernardino Freeway (probably less) but do I have the right to worry my whole family this way? What can I do about the problems of Central America in ten days, anyhow? Maybe this is only a bad dream and I'll wake up soon, safe in my own bed, my dear husband by my side. What if he should have a heart attack while I'm gone?

Our older son called last weekend from Phoenix where he lives with his wife and new baby–my first grandchild. "I'll tell Bobby why he doesn't have a grandmother when he's old enough to understand," he said. He was probably just kidding, but the irate tone of voice was real enough.

Perhaps it's symptomatic of a deep-seated Cinderella Complex, but this would have been a lot easier if I weren't all by myself. Because the rest of the group is flying out of San Francisco, I won't even meet them until midmorning in Mexico City. That is, if I can find them in the airport! I've never met any of them and I've never been to Mexico City before. I just didn't know that going off into the unknown alone was going to be so scary.

On my last Sunday at church many people wished me a safe trip and said, "we'll be praying for you." I was touched and grateful, but now the thought comes to me that when people pray for you that means you are in some kind of Trouble!

I close my eyes and try a little prayer of my own. "Please, God, take care of Dave and the rest of my family while I'm away. Don't let anyone get sick or need me when I'm not there. And please help me to remember why I am going to Nicaragua." If God is Ultimate Reality, as Dave has always told me, then certainly the search for truth must be, in some sense, the search for God. The search for truth is the reason why I am making this trip; I must know what is real. The president says we are sending money to the " Freedom Fighters" who want to overthrow the Sandinista government of Nicaragua, yet I've heard from other sources that these Freedom Fighters are mercenaries who kill innocent villagers. If my government is doing something unjust then it is my responsibility to find out about it, then to do what I can to change the situation. And yet I've only been an observer of suffering, I don't know if I have the courage to become a participant!

In spite of my panic attack, I manage to fall asleep. There's nothing like terror to wear a person out! After about an hour, I am awakened by a terrible scream, one of the classic blood curdling types. A light goes on in the back of the plane. Heads turn. Necks crane. Nothing to be seen. It must be just someone having a nightmare but it sure doesn't help my nerves any. That is the end of sleep for me. I wish I had not discovered how cowardly I really am.

I guess maybe we in the United States don't get much experience with uncontrollable situations. We are handed fear in carefully premeasured packets; the Matterhorn at Disneyland or the parachute drop at Knott's Berry Farm.

Luckily, I'm next to a window for distraction. We've been flying east so dawn can already be seen as a thin, white line on the horizon. As I watch, the line turns pale blue, then yellow, and finally red. Lightning arcs through a nest of clouds over a mountain range to the east and gradually the lights of the Mexican villages over which we have been passing are extinguished by cloud cover.

Now we are descending through the grayness. We break out of it above a marshy area dissected by a canal. The wheels touch tarmac. We are in Mexico City. I am so interested in what I'm seeing that I forget to be scared. A light mist is falling. Small square buildings on the hills beyond the airport are tinted pale gray in the soft morning light. It's beautiful and I feel encouraged.

I walk down the steps alone into a light mist. The rainy season has started. Maybe the Nicaraguan roads will be too muddy for travel. Maybe we won't be able to get to the war zone after all and we'll just stay safely in Managua.

As I leave the plane, I ask the flight attendant where the Mexicana flight from San Francisco will be arriving later in the morning. He assures me it will land at Gate A, "on the opposite side of the airport."

Armed with the confidence of one who finally knows where she's going, I negotiate customs and emerge into the airport. It is modern and beautifully decorated. I was expecting the smell and confusion of the Lima airport, but things seem much more organized here. A few men try to carry my suitcase, but a polite, "no, gracias," is enough to get me past them. After what seems like a mile of walking, though, I'm beginning to wish I'd said yes. The flight steward was right, Gate A is on the other side of the airport!

After the long walk, I am right back where I started, Gate H. When I got to Gate A, I discovered it was for domestic flights only. There seemed to be nothing to do but go back to the place where I came in and wait. Surely they will have to go through customs just as I did.

The arrival board is not working yet. Too early I guess. It's five a.m., nothing to do but sit here and wait until midmorning.

Still later

That wasn't so difficult! I found them. I finally guessed that their plane must have stopped in Guadelajara and gone through customs there and so I dragged myself and my suitcase back to Gate A again. Sure enough! Now that I'm with a group, I feel much more secure. The herd instinct, I suppose.

It is early afternoon and we are waiting in the departure lounge for the Nicaraguan airliner that will take us to Managua. Everyone is very tired from the night of traveling. Bill, a Methodist minister from Santa Rosa, is sleeping on the floor. Jon, a retired minister from Sebastopol, is sleeping sitting up. The rest of us are chatting wearily or staring glassy eyed at the walls. Two women, Kay and Debby, who are about my age are sitting across from me. Marilyn, a theology student, is with them. Hal, the refugee co-coordinator for his diocese, is talking to Evan, who I think is a writer. Kay, a retired professional woman (teacher, I think) is sorting through her purse. We had our first crisis as we went through the departure gate and she couldn't at first find her tourist card. The Mexican officials refused to be understanding about her eyesight problems (she is almost blind) and she was sent off somewhere to wait in a long line. Evan went with her and, after several anxious minutes, she found her papers.

Leticia, an American citizen who was born in Nicaragua, is sitting next to me. She left Nicaragua 30 years ago, as a teenager, but she has been back every 3 or 4 years since to visit her sisters. She will be a great help to us in understanding the changes since the Revolution.

I am trying not to think about the next part of the trip. I'm a nervous flyer under the best of conditions and I'm afraid this won't be the best of conditions. What will the airplane be like? I know the Nicaraguans can't get spare parts since the CIA mined the harbor at Corinto. They also can't import any more gasoline since the docks were destroyed last fall. What if they try to economize and don't put enough fuel in the tanks? No, that's silly. I'm sure it will be safe. It's funny how even though my <u>mind</u> questions all that I've heard in the media about the evils of Nicaragua, my <u>body</u> is in the habit of believing what I am told and I'm starting to get weak and sweaty again.

On the Nicaraguan Airliner

When we walk through the boarding gate into what is certainly the strangest looking airplane I've ever seen, I have another full-fledged panic attack. Instead of rows of seats facing forward, there is one long bench all around the outside facing inward. I'd seen something like this before–in World War II movies; you sit on the bench and hang onto a strap until it's your turn to jump. Is this a World War II war surplus plane that the Nicaraguans got from Russia? All this flashes through my mind in less than a second. As I am about to observe that the thing will never get off the ground, someone says with obvious relief, "Oh, it's a bus.

Well, it isn't exactly a bus, but the functional equivalent. It is a strange sort of vehicle that delivers us to our airplane–a perfectly normal Boeing 727. The Nicaraguan plane has been parked at a far end of the airport as if it has a contagious disease that other airplanes might catch. Although a grass mat has been substituted for carpeting at the entrance, everything looks clean and not shabby. Once seated, I begin looking around suspiciously. My fact-finding must start immediately if I am to get my job done. My eyes light first on the lettering on the front bulkhead, "No smoking in the first five rows," it says in English. Under that, the message is presumably written again, but the letters are strange. It must be Russian! But no... looking more closely, I see not Russian, but Greek. We're riding in a used Greek airliner. I feel much better!

The crew is polite and friendly. The only security was a quick electronic "frisk" as we boarded. The young man with the electronic wand gave us an apologetic smile as he waved the wand over us. Now the stewardess is walking up and down the aisle, carefully checking seatbelts. She gently reminds my seatmate, Jon, to fasten his. Things are bumping and creaking most horribly as we taxi to the end of the runway.

Takeoff is agonizingly slow! There are endless numbers of small, dust-colored, square buildings beneath us – not very far beneath us! I hope this struggle is a function of the high altitude of Mexico City, and not an indictment of the airplane. The galley looks pitifully clean and empty. I'm sure they won't feed us. They probably don't have enough food for their own people, why would they feed strangers?

Oh, but what is this? A young flight attendant with a cart of drinks. He leans over and says, with a kind smile, "Do you speak Spanish?"

"*Un poquito,*" I reply.

"Would you like something to drink?" His English is flawless. I gratefully accept an orange juice.

My mother-in -law would like these polite, clean-cut young people. And they are so touchingly young, younger than our own children.

A thick, but fragile cloud layer hangs over Central America. It makes bumpy going; however, my nervousness seems to be subsiding. Jon is telling me about his previous visits to Nicaragua. And what is this? Dinner! I haven't had anything to eat since yesterday. I am surprised. I had expected beans and rice, but instead there is lots of meat, a kind of pork, I think, with melted cheese inside; potatoes, peas and carrots, a salad, rolls, and even dessert – a peach tart.

Leticia comes up the aisle and tells us that she has been talking to a Swiss businessman who is on his way to Matagalpa, her hometown. His company, Nestle, owns 40% of the milk plant there. So here is Fact Number One–capitalism is still alive in Nicaragua: for Nestle, at least.

Now we are descending over highlands deeply dissected by parallel canyons. There are fields in a wild confusion of varied shapes and then the expanse of water that I know must be Lake Managua. The city is stretched out along its south shore. From the air Managua is tree filled and pretty, very different from the jumble of dusty slums that was Mexico City seen from above. The passengers burst into applause, not after landing, but as soon as Managua, Nicaragua is announced. The landing deserves applause, however–not a bump!

We taxi toward the terminal, a new building built of lacy cinderblock. The captain says, in a voice full of obvious pride, "Ladies and gentlemen, Managua, Nicaragua, home of Augusto Sandino! Please remain seated until the seat belt light is turned off. Thank you!"

Chapter Three

First Impressions of Managua

Stepping from the plane, the sunlight hits like a fist. Even though it is late afternoon the light is more powerful than anywhere I've been before. The air is soft, sticky and full of the smell of blossoms. Red flowered shrubs grow all around the terminal building. There are no soldiers and no guns. In Peru, our first impression had been one of fear as we walked between rows of heavily armed military guards. I thought it would be worse here, but everyone seems very relaxed. We must exchange $60 into *cordobas* before we go through customs. The young lady who makes the transaction is friendly and patient.

Is everyone here under twenty-five? The young man who stamps our passports strikes his forehead in mock despair when he sees that I've put my name in the wrong blank on my tourist card. None of us understand how to fill them out right. The problem is something involving family name and mother's last name, but the officials are good-natured about it and finally they rewrite the things for us.

The customs inspectors are equally young and good-natured. As they look through our luggage, Leticia offers one of them a tube of toothpaste. We've all brought lots of toothpaste for gifts because we've been told there is a great shortage of that commodity here.

The customs officer shakes her head sadly, "Oh, no. I couldn't take anything from you."

"But it's just a gift," says Leticia, "I brought lots of toothpaste to give to Nicaraguans because we heard it's hard to get here."

"That's true, it is scarce, but I couldn't take anything from you; it just wouldn't be right."

Outside insects drone loudly in the soft leaves of the acacia trees. The air smells wonderful. We stand on the octagonal paving stones of the parking lot and watch as our baggage is loaded into the small bus, which our host, Mike, has rented for us. Mike, a tall sandy haired young man, has come to meet us. Jon, the retired minister, tells me that Mike grew up in Brazil, the son of missionaries, and has lived in Managua about a year.

Under a tree in the parking lot is a wooden taxi stand. On it a sign says, "Welcome to Free Nicaragua. Cooperative service for taxis and hotels." Across the street, directly in front of the terminal, I see my first armed soldier. He is joking with a friend and the rifle is slung casually over his shoulder.

The bus is clean and in good repair. We slide open all the windows and start off into town while a warm breeze whips our hair. Everyone looks excited and alert. Fatigue is forgotten.

But between the airport and downtown, my new optimism begins to fade. What the trees hid from the air was some of the most dreadful housing I have ever seen. It's even worse than Peru. People seem to be living in shacks that look like chicken coops. Next we pass bombed out shells of factories. Mike explains that the central area of the city has not been rebuilt since the 1972 earthquake. It seems that Somoza took all the relief funds that came from all over the world following the earthquake, and deposited them in his own Swiss bank accounts. No wonder the housing is so bad, first the earthquake, then the Revolution, and now the Contra. How discouraging!

The center of the city is completely devastated. Many blocks are empty except for rubble and weeds. Here and there parts of buildings remain, some containing makeshift shelters where people appear to be living. Mike points out the only remaining building of any size; it is the tall, white Bank of America tower.

The bus circles the hulking shell of what was once the main cathedral and stops in Revolutionary Plaza in front of the old National Palace, now decorated with twenty foot high posters of revolutionary heroes. A militia is drilling in the square. This is the Nicaragua I was expecting and the panic begins to return. The militia group is not overwhelming in size–perhaps twenty or thirty people, but their hearty shouts chill me to the bone. Cautiously, I sneak a photo of them from inside the bus.

The group files off the bus and I follow.

"Do they mind if we watch?" I ask Mike.

"No," he says, with some surprise.

We sit down on the curb about five feet from the first row of young people. From this vantage point, I can appreciate the foolishness of my question. The militia looks more like a junior high gym class than an army.

The boys and girls, about half of them in uniform, the rest in an assortment of jeans and tee shirts, are all under eighteen and most look closer to twelve. No one, not even the boy in charge, has a weapon.

The heartiness of their shouts comes from real enthusiasm. They seem to be having fun and, like kids everywhere, obviously enjoy having an audience. Are these the hordes that are "frightening their Central American neighbors?"

Hal stops a sullen looking man who is crossing the street. Pointing to a "hero" poster two stories tall, Hal asks, "What do you think of him?"

The man shrugs. "Oh they say he's a hero, but I don't know. Maybe it's just propaganda." He gives Hal a friendly pat on the shoulder and walks on.

I think there may be a Fact here, if I can sort it out. The man sounded skeptical, but not hostile. He sounded like people in the U.S. often do when discussing politics. In his last speech, Reagan said that the Sandinistas were practicing "internal terrorism against their own people," yet this man didn't seem afraid to express a negative opinion even in the shadow of the militia. He had no way of knowing who we were. Hal's parents were born in El Salvador and Hal's Spanish is good enough that he could have been anyone, even a government agent.

Revolutionary Plaza is bounded on one side by the wrecked cathedral, another side by the battered National Palace, and on the third by a tree filled park. In this park is an eternal flame of a modern design, simple but graceful, dedicated to Carlos Fonseca Amador, the intellectual father of the Revolution. Three armed soldiers provide a ceremonial guard for the monument. The sight of them makes me nervous at first, but they chat with passers-by and don't seem especially formidable, so Kay and I stroll over for a closer look. Strewn about the base of the monument are floral bouquets of varying sizes and types. One, now quite wilted, looks like the kind of assorted flowers a child might present to a mother or teacher. There is something very sincere about those flowers. Evidently a few people still believe in heroes!

11:00 p.m.

This is the first time in about 40 hours that my body has been prone, but somehow I'm not sleepy yet. I'm writing with the aid of my pocket flashlight so as not to disturb Leticia who is my roommate. I am thankful that she and I have become friends so quickly. After all, she was born and raised in Nicaragua, so had she not moved to the United States she would be one of the people that my tax money is helping to kill. Before we turned out the light, she remarked that it seemed we had known each other a long time already. It really does.

Our hotel, called the Hotel Colon, is modest, but comfortable. Some of the rooms even have air conditioners; ours however, is not among them. We have a noisy fan and one screen-less window. Leaving the window open is taking something of a chance since this is malaria country and mosquito season, but closing the window is out of the question even though Mike warned us that the Cloroquin we are taking does not prevent malaria - it just suppresses the symptoms. We will have to rely on the Sandinista public health system for protection. One of their early health projects was to mobilize great numbers of volunteers to go out into the countryside and to hand out medicines to all of the Nicaraguans at the same time. Only in this way could the malaria parasite be eliminated from the entire population before reinfection could occur. Let's hope no mosquitoes have sneaked in from Honduras!

The cot I'm lying on has a mattress about half and inch thick on top of bare springs. Every move I make sends loud squeaks through the room. Added to the melody of the fan and the steady beat of the air conditioner next door, we have a virtual orchestra. I'm really quite comfortable, though after dinner and a shower. There is only cold water, but in this weather, who cares?

I wasn't hungry enough to order a whole dinner so Kay gave me a couple bites of hers. It was very good; a stew of sliced cabbage with chicken and tomato, rice and beans on the side. I drank a glass of papaya juice, which was utterly divine.

Now I should be going to sleep. We have a heavy schedule ahead of us. Mike outlined it for us at dinner. Next weekend we are supposed to go up to the war zone on the Honduran border. Well...maybe I'll get sick and won't be able to go. Perhaps if I eat some of the lettuce that we aren't supposed to eat, just by mistake of course, I'll be sick and will have to wait here at the nice, safe hotel. Certainly there are lots of facts to be found right here in Managua without risking my neck, aren't there? Oh, I am such a cowardly custard! Why did I come here anyway? I would turn off the flashlight, but as soon as I am alone in the dark, I start thinking about Dave. I hope he isn't lonely. I hope he isn't missing me too much. Missing. Reminds me of that movie. Oh, no, don't even think about that!

Chapter Four

We Explore the Countryside and Attend a Campesino Mass

Sunday, May 20

I know I didn't sleep long, yet I am wide-awake at 7:30, and anxious to start Finding Facts. The first thing I find is breakfast: toasted French bread with marmalade, rice, beans, scrambled eggs, and more of that terrific papaya juice. There is so much food that we divide orders for 6 between the 12 of us so as not to waste anything. As we eat, classical music is playing from somewhere. The room that functions as both lobby and dining room is actually a kind of breezeway connecting the front of the hotel with the rooms beyond. A warm wind flows through the room; soft and very pleasant.

The hotel itself is all on one floor and is actually a cluster of several small buildings grouped around red tiled courtyards. This same large square tile extends into the rooms as well. The center of each courtyard is a large, sunken rectangle of earth planted with palms and feral green houseplants and carpeted by long, soft bladed grass that lies spread across the ground like mermaid's hair. I suspect that in rainy weather it looks even more like mermaid's hair, because the drain spouts from the roof are all pointed in the direction of these verdant rectangles.

Now that it's daylight, I can get a better idea of where we are. The hotel is in a nice, middle class neighborhood in the hills south of downtown. The streets are paved and there are curbs and sidewalks. The houses are modern and the lawns are green. Except for the message "Viva Sandino" neatly stenciled on walls and utility poles, this could be suburban Los Angeles.

That impression is further reinforced a few block later as we pass a MacDonald's, complete with golden arches. Then, very quickly, we are in the country surrounded by planted and plowed fields. Pale, long horned cattle graze by the side of the road. A large billboard says, "better to loose a minute than a life" and illustrates the point with a picture of a car carelessly passing a bus on a curve and heading for certain doom in the shape of an oncoming truck.

Now we seem to be in a volcanic wasteland. Jagged black boulders straggle off in all directions. Huge clouds of steam churn into the air from the truncated shape of, what Mike tells us,is the Masaya Volcano. When he said we were going to visit a volcano, I thought he meant extinct!

We stop at the gates of the Masaya Volcano National Park. Everything seems tidy and well maintained. Again, I feel as if I were at home. The young park ranger in the gatehouse could easily be a U.S. Dept. of Interior employee. She asks us if we could give a ride to some Germans who wanted to go up to the volcano. She motions in the direction of two, blond haired young men. Of course, we are glad to; the better to Find Facts, m'dear!

As the bus struggles upward at a 30-degree angle toward the billowing steam, we discover (in a tri-lingual conversation) that the young men are mechanics, here as part of an international corps of volunteers.

"Did you find what you expected in Nicaragua?" someone asks them.

"Yes, and more! It is very exciting to be part of this," says one.

"Right now we are building houses for the people who must move from the border areas," says the other, "Next week we go back to Germany, but in November we will volunteer again for either one or two years."

The bus rounds one final curve and we disembark in a parking lot in front of the steaming caldera. The noise is something like a cross between the ocean and a strong wind. We all go over to the edge and when I stand up on the stone wall to take a picture down into the seemingly bottomless steam vent, I feel my lungs constrict and refuse to work.

"Poison gas," Mike explains, "Sulfuric acid and nitrous oxide."

Amazingly, though, the air is alive with twittering shapes. Thousands of parrots that have adapted their lungs to life inside the volcano nest in the cliffs where they are safe from predators.

Shouting over the sound of the steam, Mike says, "Before the Revolution this was known as Somoza's Brazier because the National Guard brought his political enemies up here and threw then in."

I look down into the terrible chasm. It would be easy enough to throw someone in all right, if you had enough help. It's a straight shot right down there. I shudder.

It's good to know, though, that this volcano, which was once a source of terror for Nicaraguans, is now a source of pride. We meet an elderly couple on the steps to the jagged summit. They give us a welcoming smile when Leticia tells them we are Americans.

"What do you think of our volcano?" The lady asks shyly.

"It's amazing," I say, "I've never seen anything like it before."

They look very pleased and wish us good luck as we part. Behind us, a fresh billow fills the entire crater with steam.

I decide to sit here, half way up the trail, and write for a while. The rest of the group has gone on. It is very peaceful. The wind is strong and the view, tremendous. On the far shore of Lake Managua, I can see the sharply conical shapes of Momotombo and Little Momotombo. Mike tells us that the Italians are building a geothermal energy project on Momotombo, which is also an active volcano. The project will make Nicaragua not only energy self-sufficient but also energy exporting within 5 years.

Soft gray clouds scud across the sky. Then suddenly the tranquility of the morning is shattered by the sound of gunfire. Is it just practice or is it (as the kids say) "for reals?" In any case, it isn't close so I won't worry about it yet.

Two more tour groups of Americans have disembarked from buses. They puff up steps below me, joking about aerobics and asking the names of things. As they pass me, I stand up and follow them to the summit where I find that some members of our group have been talking to the first Cubans we've met, two men and a woman. They say they are doctors and they certainly do have the look of professional people (whatever that means.) They are middle aged, not what I think of as military types. But after they leave, Mike says that our government counts them as military advisors. Since all Cubans must undergo military training in their youth, all Cubans are automatically considered "military personnel."

Masaya, and a mini-lecture on Nicaraguan government

On the road to Masaya, Mike uses the time to orient us to the structure of post-Revolutionary Nicaraguan government:

"The Junta is the executive branch. It is made up of three people; two of them are Sandinistas, Daniel Ortega and Dr. Sergio Ramirez. The third is a conservative, a member of one of the opposition parties, Rafael Cordova Rivas. Under these three are 40 cabinet ministers, some are Sandinistas, and some belong to other parties. The Council of State is the legislative branch and shares power with the executive branch. There are 52 members in the Council of State elected by their various groups. Now representation is by interest groups, like unions or professional organizations, but this

41

will change to geographical representation after the November election."

As we enter the town of Masaya, we pass beneath the formidable hulk of an old colonial fort, squatting on a hill overlooking the whole city. Mike points it out to us saying, "During the last days of the Revolution, just a week before the Triumph, Somoza's National Guard lobbed artillery shells on Masaya from that fort. You will see a lot of destruction in the city.

We did, too. There are many empty lots, some with shattered walls still remaining. Reconstruction is proceeding, though, despite of an apparent shortage of materials. In several places, I see walls made of the straightened out sides of oil drums.

The bus drops us off at the market so that we can browse and talk to people. Leticia and I set off among the new corrugated iron stalls. The market is crowded, but clean and well organized. The proprietor of one stall tells us that the rent is 3 cordobas (about 10 cents) a day and that a government official collects the rent daily. The salespeople are all friendly and willing to engage in conversation, but there is no hard sell of the kind I've encountered in markets in other countries. They seem happy to answer questions about the merchandise, but they don't initiate anything. Leticia and I each buy an embroidered dress for about $15.

We spend an hour in the market talking to people and photographing willing children. The people seem mostly to be quite happy with their new government. No one reports any repression. Everyone is so relaxed and friendly that I forget for the moment that this is supposed to be hostile territory.

Dogs wander freely, threading their way between legs. They look much better than Peruvian dogs. Not only are they fatter but they don't slink with their tails between their legs. I even see people sharing their lunches with them.

As we head back toward the bus, Leticia buys a giant green pod, about a foot long. She opens it and inside are lima bean shaped green things on a scale with the pod. We nibble on them and find they have a strange, astringent taste. Leticia has forgotten what they are called.

The bus takes us out of Masaya and climbs a hill into another community known as Monimbo. This is a neighborhood of small but sturdy adobe houses. It has long been noted for its high quality arts and crafts.

"This was an area of fierce fighting in the early days of the Revolution," Mike tells us.

We stop in front of a corner house. It bears a plaque telling how Somoza's National Guard used it as a head-quarters until the people of the neighborhood rose up en masse, stormed the post and captured the weapons. This was an important early victory for the Revolution.

Grenada and Lake Nicaragua

In the country, we pass fields filled with large herds of the pale cattle. Evan tells me they are Texas Long Horns crossed with Indian Brahmas. They are well suited to the climate.

Another amazing thing I have discovered–the fence posts are growing! They really are growing! The new ones have little green shoots coming from their tops, the older ones are full-fledged shrubs, and the really old ones don't look like fence posts at all, they look like a row of trees!

We see new farmhouses being constructed from cinderblock. On the hillsides, banana trees grow in little clumps. Sometimes we pass trucks filled with people who often wave to us.

Grenada is a lovely, white colonial town on the shore of Lake Nicaragua. In the center of town, a block from the main square is a billboard that says, in Spanish, *"If your enemy is hungry, feed him. Overcome evil with good. Romans 12:20*

I thought these people were supposed to be atheistic Communists!

As Leticia, Kay, and I wander around town, people meet our eyes and smile. In the admittedly short time I've been here, I have noticed an atmosphere that I have not experienced before in a Latin country. It is something to do with dignity and equality. It is a feeling that you get from waiters, shopkeeper, and government officials; nobody acts either servile or officious. It's hard to quantify as a "Fact" but it's real. One fact I can attest to though, I've not seen even one beggar yet.

We buy *cajeta*, a kind of milk candy, from an old lady. It is delicious and she is pleased when I tell her so.

We have lunch at a restaurant, more veranda than building, actually, on the shore of Lake Nicaragua. The lake is very large, too large to see across, and in it lurk the only fresh water sharks in the world. This fact has not seemed to deter swimmers, however, and we watch families enjoy a Sunday at the beach while we eat.

The food is marvelous; a big steak covered with onions, platinos, salad (I don't eat it), beets, rice, and bread. Sergio, our bus driver sits between Hal and me. He tells us that his two brothers live in the U.S. but that he has no desire to join them.

After lunch, I stroll along the beach alone and feel very safe. Was it really less than 24 hours ago that I was terrified at the thought of venturing out of the hotel alone?

Families are having picnics under the trees along the shore. One family with a new Japanese camper and station wagon could have been a typical American family in a TV ad. Now Dad and Grandpa sit in lawn chairs by the camper watching the children play. On this lovely Sunday afternoon, it's hard to remember that this is a country under siege. There are even rumors that this tranquil lake has been mined.

Back to Managua

Once more we are on the road, traveling through an area of banana and mango orchards. A billboard advertises the Conservative Democrat Party, a major opposition party to the Sandinistas. Evidently, they have the right to advertise their dissent.

We pass two pharmaceutical manufacturing plants. They are large and modern. The government has made the production of medicines a high priority. Low priority has been given to things like pop bottles. Bottles are so scarce that when you buy pop "to go" they pour it into a plastic bag and keep the bottle. People walking down the sidewalk drinking out of baggies are a common sight.

Back at the hotel we have half and hour to shower and change for Mass. I lift up the lid of the toilet and there is a cockroach at least two inches long. I didn't know they made them that big! I flush quickly and he disappears but I still feel squeamish. I know that guy can swim and he'll be back!

Campesino Mass in the Barrio Riguerro

Now we are in the neighborhood where the National Guard shot the U.S. reporter in 1979, in an act that so shocked our nation that Somoza's loss of American support was assured. All seems peaceful enough now. This is a poor neighborhood, however the houses, though small, are tidy. The streets are lined with big trees. Utility poles attest to electric service. This is another Fact I have found. In our travels today I have seen lots of new, cement utility poles and several sewer projects. This is amazing to me because we never saw any evidence of such services in the poor neighborhoods of Peru and Bolivia.

Our reason for being here on this Sunday evening is to attend what is called "a *Campesino* Mass. "*Campesino*" simply means "someone from the country" but it has come to mean "poor" or "ordinary" people. Obviously, we are not in "the country" but in an urban semi-slum. The title means something like "poor people's Mass".

We walk toward the church building to the accompaniment of booming electronic bells. The people in the streets are well dressed and seem animated and cheerful. Here too, the dogs look well fed. A large German shepherd sits in the street in front of the church. He looks as if he came to the right place because just behind him is a statue of St. Francis of Assisi petting a wolf.

A friendly, handsome young man greets us in front of the church. He is probably in his early twenties. He wears a Sandinista beret and scarf and a blue shirt with a military cut. Though it isn't quite a uniform, it does set him apart as some kind of leader. He shakes hands with all of us and then we proceed inside the sanctuary.

The building is large and new, but not imposing in the sense of a cathedral. From the outside it is distinctly "low profile," however inside there is a feeling of height provided by the conical ceiling and skylight. The pews are arranged in a semicircle. If the exposed beams were laminated wood rather than structural steel, I could think I was in a modern church at hone. I could, that is, until I turn and see the murals on the back walls. They are scenes of revolution and struggle. In one, an armored soldier on horseback is trampling a priest and several peasants. The soldier suggests no specific time or place but is clearly an allegorical figure suggesting tyranny in all its forms. Another of the murals centers around a Christ figure, a peasant boy of 12 or 14, standing before a firing squad composed of a trio of militaristic monsters with twisted features and claws and tentacles instead of feet. Behind the boy are more peasants including a young woman, the lower half of her face obscured by a red and black Sandinista scarf in the manner of the revolutionary fighters.

We look for seats. There is plenty of space. I wonder if the Mass is going to be attended mostly by North Americans? There are lots of us here, maybe as many as a hundred. I recognize some of them from the volcano this morning. We seem to outnumber the Nicaraguans.

The prelude, played by guitars and drums, is beginning. Now I see what the Sandinista's uniform was for, he's a musician and evidently the leader of the band. The music is accomplishing what the deafening electronic church bells failed to do. The church is filling up with Nicaraguans. Now they outnumber us rather decisively. There seems to be standing room only.

The music continues and soon everyone is singing. The middle aged Nicaraguan lady across the aisle from me is weeping silently as she sings. Tears are making trails down her lined cheeks. Is she remembering a child lost in the war? I don't understand all the words of the song, but I understand enough to know that it is about the Revolution.

Earlier, Leticia told me that she went to high school with the priest who is now the senior pastor at this church. His name is Father Molina and I gather he is quite famous.

"The man is a saint," she told me, "He dedicates his life to the poor."

He does have a saintly appearance–a kind of radiant warmth. After an opening prayer, he introduces a guest -a priest from Chile.

The Chilean priest, an old man with a fringe of white hair, gives a short speech and concludes by saying, "I come to Nicaragua to breathe free."

The young Sandinista also serves as lector. He reads a passage from the Scriptures and I recognize the verse, *"In my Father's house are many mansions. I go to prepare a place for you."*

Father Molina speaks again. There is more music and rising emotion. I feel that the emotion is, in a sense, "orchestrated," but no more than at the Crystal Cathedral, or other such institution. At least this does seem to be honest emotion in that it taps a source that is already present in the people. The tears of the lady across the aisle flowed from the beginning of the service; no one had to elicit them.

This is an intensely romantic revolution, no getting around that, but given the youth of the participants and the unbelievable odds of teenagers against tanks, it's no wonder. I am reminded of Hungary–1956. Maybe that's why I have trouble seeing Russian influence as important here. These people don't really have much in common with the ossified Russian society. Kay spent several months in Russia as a student and hated it. She says the atmosphere here is nothing like Russia; no fear, no repression, no constant military presence.

What I hear is fiercely nationalistic. I do not hear the name of Marx or Lenin; all I hear is Sandino, Sandino, Sandino.

Now we have come to a part of the service where the dead heroes of the Revolution are honored. As each name is read everyone calls out, "Presente!" It is deeply moving. The people know that they owe their freedom to those who have died, would they betray that trust by selling out to Russia?

On the other hand, if we keep the pressure on them and take steps to prevent our allies from selling them weapons to protect themselves, where else can they turn?

Father Molina speaks of "our children, tortured and murdered..." I look around at the lovely faces of the young people and remember the tales I have heard of torture under Somoza. These are really people, not statistics. These are just kids–kids like my own.

The young Sandinista is speaking again. He addresses the North American guests directly and in English saying, "we need your help. We wish your health. We love you."

Two North American pastors from other groups go to the front and reply in Spanish with wishes for brotherhood. Father Molina invites all the North American visitors to come forward.

We make a large double circle around the altar and sing "We Shall Over Come." The song is followed by the "Kiss of Peace," when everyone shakes hands or embraces. Most of the North Americans stay in the group around the altar and embrace their friends. Several of us, however go back to the congregation to embrace Nicaraguans. I will not forget the touch of their bodies–warm and real. I won't forget the eager trust of the children; the little girls who throw their arms around my waist, the grandmotherly warmth and strength of the elderly ladies, many of who are weeping.

Please, God, don't let mine be a Judas Kiss!

We share the Lord's Prayer, in English and Spanish simultaneously, and then we come forward for Communion.

Returning to the back pew where I had been sitting, I suddenly remember that in the several times I've gotten up, I've left my purse sitting wide open on the end of the pew. It contains my tape recorder, my camera, all my money, my credit card, my passport and my ticket home–all the fragile things, in short, that make me different from these people.

But returning, I see with relief that everything is still there. My privileged status is secure.

Following the service there is a "coffee hour" in the courtyard, only it is too hot for coffee, so fruit juice is sold at a small stand. The musical group moves outside, too, and begins to play while four girls, 12 or 14 years old, dressed in bright blue peasant costumes, perform a folk dance. They smile shyly as they go through their carefully practiced routine.

As our bus jolts back to the hotel through the Barrio Riguerro, I note that each tiny house has a TV screen glowing within like a pale, blue-white hearth. What is being watched? In Peru we used to go to the corner restaurant and watch old U.S. made movies and adventure shows. Seeing those images while surrounded by the squalor of a Lima street corner, I began to realize how constantly we are on display to the rest of the world. In almost every store and coffee shop sits a TV and from that TV flows a constant stream of images of luxury and ease, speaking eloquently of a basic unfairness. The average Latin American knows he works harder than we do, why then doesn't he have cars and huge homes? Aren't TV sets massive "exporters of revolution to the third world?" Didn't Reagan himself, as an actor, participate in this exportation of revolution?

Dinner at the hotel consists of lettuce, tomato, "porcupine" meat balls (hamburger and rice), cooked carrots and cooked jicama in a sweet buttery sauce, fried bananas cooked in sugar, toast and chi cha (which is a fruit drink with a strong honey flavor.) My teeth are beginning to ache from so much sugar.

I have "found" at least two Facts today:

1. Fact - I have seen children in poor neighborhoods wearing eyeglasses. I never saw that in Peru or Bolivia. Interpretation-this could mean either that children in Nicaragua have inferior eyes or, that someone is taking better care of the medical needs of children here than of children in Peru and Bolivia.

2. Fact - People stand up straight and look you in the eye. The people that we met in the streets and market places speak of "our" Revolution.

Interpretation - The body language seems to indicate a new confidence and pride. They don't feel like victims anymore.

Chapter Five

The Press:
From *La Prensa* To La *Barricada*
With A Stop At The Women's Group

Monday morning

We drift, a few at a time, into the breezeway/dining room with its blue and white checked tablecloths looking homey and cheerful in the morning sunlight. While we eat our eggs, rice, beans, papaya, and coffee, Leticia and Evan discuss the changes the Revolution has brought in the treatment of domestic servants.

"They can't call them 'maids' any more," Leticia, says, "They must call them 'employees' and they have to have one day a week off and a minimum wage."

"That doesn't sound too radical," Evan says, chewing thoughtfully.

"Not to us, but you can imagine my friends with seven maids throwing up their hands."

"Sure," Evan agrees, "when I lived in Guatemala you just went out and got a girl from the country and took her to live at your house. If you brought home guests at 2:00 am, you wanted food for them, you'd go wake her up and say, 'get up now and cook!'"

"Yes, it was like that here, too before the Revolution," says Leticia, buttering a slice of toasted French bread,

"It was a terrible thing. People would take a peasant girl from the country and promise to educate her and, of course, they never did. She was just like a slave. But they can't do this anymore. Now there is a quitting time. There are regular hours and medical benefits. That why a lot of rich people don't like the Revolution."

We set off in the bus again, this time on our way to La Prensa—the bastion of the opposition. On the way, we pass a line of perhaps a dozen people waiting for gas for their stoves.

"That's what some people will point to as a failure of the Revolution," says Leticia, "that people have to wait in line for gas. But isn't it better to wait in line for gas for your stove than to have no stove? When I lived here the poor people cooked on three stones with a stick of wood."

We are stopping at a shopping mall. It looks just like a shopping mall in Southern California. I could think I was at home. One thing is different though, no mannequins displaying women's jeans, just a form fitted under them.

"They can't use women's bodies to sell merchandise anymore," Leticia tells me as we stroll through the mall "It's a new law that the Women's Organization succeeded in getting through. Oh, you see it sometimes, but they are trying to stop using women in that way."

We go into a bookstore. I love bookstores and I am eager to find some Facts in this one. The fact is that there is one whole wall of books by Marx, Lenin, and Engles. A poster of Chernenko stares gloomily down on me. I buy a book of Latin American poetry and find my hands shaking in the presence of so much Communism. So it's true, the Nicaraguans are Communists!

But wait, Mike is telling us that this is not an average bookstore. This is the Marxist-Leninist Bookstore. Well, I'll check out some others for myself and see. Funny how I'm so willing, anxious even, to find Facts which will support the position my government has taken. I was <u>glad</u> to see the poster of Chernenko because it makes me feel so safe to think that my government knows best. It relieves me of the responsibility of having to think about things for myself. How nice if I could just go home and lie in the sun and read a magazine and not have to think about politics anymore!

But on my way out of the bookstore, I notice something else. Even in this avowedly Marxist store, a large share of the books are practical books about public health in peasant societies. These books come from Cuba, but where else can the Nicaraguans find models for such things? Not from us, certainly. I can't imagine that our medical community would be interested in promoting "barefoot" doctors or midwives. The kind of high-tech stuff we publish is useless in third world countries. Where else has low cost mass health care been successfully used besides Cuba and China? This is something to check on when I get home.

We arrive at the entrance to _La Prensa_, the opposition (to the Sandinistas) press that has been championed by Reagan. It is flanked on one side by the Coca-Cola Company and on the other side by the Bank of America. The entire compound is surrounded by a high wall topped by barbed wire. We are checked at the gate by a guard. The building itself is a modest cinderblock structure. We are ushered into an air-conditioned office and, after we are seated, the associate editor, Roberto Cardenal, a balding and very white man, enters. His manner is bored and somewhat condescending. He speaks to us in English:

"The F.S.L.N., that is the Sandinista Party, took control soon after the Revolution. Some points that they have not fulfilled are that they still have sixty percent of the vote in the Council of State - that is not democratic. They have set up tribunals independent of the Supreme Court and the state sector of the economy is growing. If your workers accuse you of decapitalization, that is selling off your machinery and equipment or allowing your farms or factories to run down, your business can be taken over by the government.

"Sixteen days ago a newspaper man was put in jail. Certain words were put in his mouth..."

We saw this on the TV. news last night. What the arrested reporter was saying was that there was a CIA. representative at every editorial meeting of _La Prensa_. I had looked hard into the TV screen as if I could pull the truth from his face with my eyes. He didn't look under duress, but how could I tell? Here is a clear point of conflict and I have no way of knowing who is telling the truth: the reporter on TV, or this man in front of me.

"Here is one of our stories that was censored. It is a letter from the Bishops against the Revolution. Make no mistake we don't like Americans here. We want a Nicaragua without American or Soviet influence. The Soviets are behind all this work in El Salvador."

He continues in this vein for some time when Leticia asks permission to ask a question. He nods a curt assent.

"Are you saying, then, that the Contras are the answer? Are they the people who are going to give freedom?"

"Well, you are such a wise person, you already know all the answers," Mr. Cardenal replies sarcastically. You can feel the shock in the room at his arrogant reply.

He goes on, "People are more hungry now than in Somoza's time. There is less medicine, less doctors. We Social Democrats want to have social change but with freedom. We prefer to be hungry lions roaming free than well-fed lions in cages..."

Am I right in hearing two contradictory statements there? I don't think I want to challenge him, though!

Kay asks, "Can you think of some existing country that operates along the lines you want to see for Nicaragua?"

"Yes, Costa Rica."

I could point out that Costa Rica has no history of repression and is also under populated, but I don't think he would listen to me.

"War is being used to take away freedoms..."

Then why don't we stop the war and remove the excuse?

"We believe that there should not be conscription. If the army is called 'Sandinista' then you can raise that reason not to serve. Would you join a Republican Party army?"

"What changes in government would make it acceptable to you?"

He pulls his jacket over his shoulders. The air conditioning is cold and loud.

"No identification between government and the Sandinista political party. We think it is wrong for the C.D.S. to distribute food. They pressure you if you do not go to their political meetings, then you don't get your food ration card."

"Must everyone go to these meetings to get a card?"

"Well, someone in the household must. And now if you will excuse me, I must meet with the Swiss ambassador."

We thank him for the interview and all rise to leave. On the way out, Evan asks him if it is true that the CIA does come to _La Prensa_ for meetings.

He smiles without warmth. "How do I know? Maybe some of _you_ are from the CIA."

The Women's Organization

The headquarters of the National Association of Women (AMNLAE) is housed in what was once someone's very luxurious home. It is one of the houses abandoned by the friends of Somoza when they left the country after the Revolution. The ceilings and many of the walls are paneled in beautiful wood parquet. The living room is now a reception room where women and their children are waiting. People are coming and going from the outside to interior rooms, which are apparently used as offices.

As we are ushered towards what was once the bedroom wing, we pass women seated at desks interviewing other women. It looks like a social agency in the U.S. except that the posters on the walls are hand lettered and there are no stacks of brochures.

As we await the director, Mike explains that this organization was begun unofficially during Somoza's time as a group for mothers whose children had disappeared. The focus of this group is less on individual rights than on social rights. Health and education are their main focus. They are represented in the Council of State.

The director enters the room. She is in her mid or late twenties, very pretty with long dark hair. She is wearing a neatly tailored plaid blouse and designer jeans. She begins by telling us the history of AMNLAE through a translator:

"Our group began before the Revolution. For our first meeting the organizers had rented a movie theater. Only 2 women showed up. One of them got up on stage and said, 'This is indeed a great event because we are made aware that we have not done what we should have done.' The next time the hall that was rented was not big enough to hold everyone because the organizers had talked to many people. We analyzed our problems and decided that the main problem was Somoza.

"Women have had a full part in the Revolution from the beginning. We were not relegated to taking care of the wounded but we fought at the barricades. We have earned a full part in society. Our organization is named for the first woman to die in the Revolution. She made a lot of sacrifices from her social background to be with the people.

"Traditionally women have never had training to be leaders, but now that we are being attacked by terrorist bands financed by the U.S., women must take on more responsibility, so we have established a woman's rural training center to learn fertilizers and things like how to do financial organization. We have been establishing day care centers, but the Contra attack them."

She smiles sadly, "Women at the border are daily joining our organization of Mothers of Heroes and Martyrs."

She means "Mothers of the Dead."

"We do not want war. We prefer that our boys not be at the border with guns, but be in school or playing sports. We see the pain in the eyes of the mothers. But at this moment to defend the Revolution is to defend life.

"Through our representation on the Council of State, three of our proposals have been made law. The first is the Law of Adoption. This is important because we have many orphans. Before the Revolution, Somoza was the leading businessman in adoptions. He sold children to couples overseas. Now our new laws say that it is more important for an adopting family to give love than to have money.

"Our second new law is the Law of Human Relations. Between men, women and children there used to be only paternal rights. Our new law tries to correct that inequality. In most of Latin America, the woman has the major responsibility for the children and the man has all the rights.

"Our third new law is the Law of Nurture. It defines how to demand child support from an absent father and also the responsibility of children for aged parents. One part of the law that was much discussed concerns the value of the work a woman does at home. Our purpose is not that men should cook and wash, but to give more freedom to both men and women."

I wish she would expand on this point, but she doesn't.

"In this country we have a Night Watch to protect the neighborhood from attack by Contra. In Managua 80% of these are women. Women have also taken a great part in the Literacy Campaign. Sixty percent of the teachers are women.

"Before the Revolution to be a good woman you had to be a good cook, housekeeper, and lover. Now the Revolution has opened other doors for women. We asked a woman who is now head of a cooperative what the Revolution meant to her. She said 'before the revolution I could eat if my husband brought me food. Now I can produce and I have my own money. I no longer put up with his beatings. I know I should not allow it, but I have mercy on him because I know he received a certain formation from the past.' We are trying to change these things but mental frameworks cannot be torn up by tearing up a piece of paper. This is our struggle.

"Some other new laws we have passed are that it is now forbidden to use women's bodies for advertising. Before it was very common to see a woman in a bathing suit advertise beer or tires.

"Also we have now outlawed prostitution. By this, I don't mean we no longer have any prostitution, but we hope that will come about when we have economic opportunity for all. Before the Revolution, it was the business of the National Guard to run houses of prostitution. Now we have opened retraining centers for these women so they can have new jobs. When we see where women are still working as prostitutes we start study circles and try to see what other work is open to them. We don't believe that they are prostitutes because they want to be, but because they have no other work. This also is a result of the aggression we are suffering. We will have to close down some of our factories because at this point we have not been able to send out our crops of coffee and cotton because our harbors are mined. We must spend our resources on defense."

Of course, I have no way of knowing if her assessment of the economic ills of the country is accurate or just a handy excuse. But isn't this one more reason for our government to stop its attack on Nicaragua? It seems to me that what we are doing is uniting the people behind the Sandinistas and providing a handy excuse for any of their failures. If we really believe that our system is better, why don't we trust it enough to allow honest competition?

She wipes her long hair out of her face and tucks a strand behind her ear as she continues. "I am asking not for an invasion of Marines who bring bombs to kill our children, but an invasion of people to help us. The bombs that the soldiers throw at us are taken from the tax money of the people. This is not Grenada. Here our people have a long history of struggle. We will fight to the end, but a war would be foolish. We are only two and a half million people. We are not a vital interest of the United States.

"We know we are not perfect. We have made many mistakes, but the important thing is we are trying to raise the standard of living of the people. Education is no longer only for a privileged few; it is for all. We have created health centers, but we cannot do all that we want to do because we are under attack.

"We are not afraid for you to talk to the opposition parties even though they will tell you many lies. You have been told that we violate the rights of Miskitu Indians, but no one mentions that trans-national mining companies used these people and ruined their lungs. No one speaks out about the many Indians who have been killed by the government of Guatemala."

The question is asked, "Are you supplying arms to the Salvadoran rebels as we have been told?"

"At no time will we deny that we support the struggle of the Salvadoran people but we do not send arms. We have no common border with El Salvador. No proof has ever been given of Nicaragua sending arms to them."

Debby wants to know, "Do you also serve women of the middle class?"

"We are for all women. One of our projects is to help people know more about their own bodies through education. We think this will help combat some forms of irresponsibility. For instance, men used to try to prove what men they were by having children with many women. Now we have a law that all children are equal, inside or outside of marriage, and that they must be provided for. We understand the liberation of women as connected to the rights of all people."

"What are your laws regarding abortion?"

"Abortion is illegal in Nicaragua. Women here do not feel that it is an important problem. In order to have a new law the people must ask for the new law. Here 98% of our people are religious. They do not want abortion. We now have free family planning clinics, but not abortion. Last year we opened our first women's hospital. We try to give special attention to the diseases of women. But while we are at war the Contra destroy our schools and our clinics. Now it is a double effort to try to rebuild everything."

Monday Afternoon

We stop at a sidewalk cafe for fruit juice and I just look around for a few minutes, trying to observe daily life. There is a lot of traffic, much more than I had expected given gas rationing. There are lots of trucks and private cars, most of them quite new and nice. Many of them are Japanese. Large new German buses provide mass transportation.

On the surface things look much more prosperous than Peru but, of course, Central America is less remote. The buildings of this cafe appear newly painted and the flowerbeds are neatly tended. We've been moving around the country for two and a half days now and I still have seen no beggars, neither have I felt a high degree of militarization. I have seen only two trucks containing soldiers (only three soldiers in one of the trucks.) I have seen no armored personnel carriers of the type that patrol the streets of Lima and the only tank I have seen was in a museum.

At The Office of *La Barricada*

This newspaper, the official voice of the Sandinistas, is also behind a guarded gate. This one is less officious than the one at *La Prensa*, however. Here there is no barbed wire, but there is a high wall with spikes set in the top.

The large, bare lobby, which looks like it was a factory once, is dominated by huge portraits of Revolutionary heroes. These are touchingly human and show those dead heroes as sensitive young men. Here is one grinning engagingly; there one appears to be dreaming idealistic dreams.

Most of the folks here are young and have that open, easy smile that seems almost a trademark of the Sandinistas. A girl, whom I take to be a secretary, ushers us into a bare conference room. She is quietly pretty and wears jeans and an Izod shirt. She looks as if she might be working on a college newspaper, but it turns out that she is the editor in charge of the international division of the newspaper. She greets us with a shy smile and tells us, through Mike's translation, that despite appearances, this is the largest newspaper in Nicaragua. She leans against a cupboard and begins, in Spanish:

"Our country has never had good training for journalists. It is also hard to get paper and ink. It is a miracle we are able to get this paper printed since our machines are very old and in poor condition. Finally, now we have one new printing press. It is wonderful!

She smiles and a dimple winks in her cheek.

"Everyone here is young. Our director is only 28 and some of our new reporters are only 18. We are experimenting with what style to use so that we can become a better newspaper. We are learning as we grow.

"What is the role of a newspaper in a revolution? Some say it should be propaganda, others say education. We think we should be as honest as possible about what is happening in the country. We report the complaints that people have and we try to help them to think and develop their own criteria. That is very difficult.

"In religion we never seek confrontation, but let the communities speak their voice. For international news, we use the news agencies. We are trying to break through the blockade of disinformation about us, but that is difficult for a small, poor country. There are about 9 other newspapers in the country. They publish on a weekly basis.

The question is asked, "do you publish opposition?"

"We try to but usually they won't talk to us.

"What percentage of your staff is female?"

"We have about 60% women editors, but in the areas like the presses, it is all men. Marketing and personnel are all women."

"Do you think there would be an advantage in letting *La Prensa* print anything it wants to and letting the people choose?"

"When the Revolution first triumphed we had no censorship. Then the CIA started its attacks on bridges on the northern frontier. Then we had to have information restriction for military purposes. Then the attack began on the economic system in order to destabilize the government. Having lived through civil war, the people know what shortages are, so when *La Prensa* prints rumors that there will be shortages of a certain item, this causes people to buy more than they need and it causes speculators to buy large quantities in order to drive up the prices. When this is happening the internal news...[I think she means, *La Prensa*] ... takes pictures of long lines and says people are hungry in Nicaragua. It does work. It is a way to destabilize a country. This information, which is not true, can cause panic.

"In spite of this however, now the censorship only applies to military information, not economic. As journalists, we don't like censorship, but we are willing to do what ever we must to keep our country ours. But I don't think that now, 5 years after the Revolution, that censorship is necessary. People know now what is really happening and they don't believe those rumors anymore.

"Now the Bishops are refusing to say Mass for the Sandinistas who have died. When the Bishops said that we must have negotiations with the Contra, a position not even taken by the right wing, we thought that attack deserved a counter attack. Some of the Bishops who supposedly signed the Christmas letter were not even in the country at the time. First, the Bishops say, "don't pick up weapons to defend yourselves," then they say to welcome the attackers into our midst. The Revolution is not going to take any steps against the Bishops, but it has a right to respond to their opinions with opinion of its own."

I am surprised to see how she maintains her air of well-bred gentleness despite her fiery words.

"We see ourselves as a tool for helping the people to understand the elections. Nicaragua does not have a history of voting. Some people are not interested and others think that having elections will mean surrendering the Revolution. We will print the programs of all the parties."

"Are you supported by the F.S.L.N. [Sandinistas]?"

"*Barricada* does not receive money from the F.S.L.N. We are independent and maintain ourselves. We sell subscriptions and advertising. We also publish books."

On the wall is posted a big map of Nicaragua. As we leave the room Mike shows Leticia and me where Ocotal is. We are going there this weekend. He says it is a prime target and has been attacked many times. The bridge has been blown up three times thus cutting off the only road connecting it to the rest of the country. It is in a sort of panhandle area surrounded on three sides by Honduras, that is why the Contra and the CIA. want to use this area as a provisional Contra government.

Oh, no. Here comes the panic again. There has been a major push this month by the Contra. They have mined roads and bridges. There are 8,000 Contra out there in the hills waiting to torture and kill. Oh, God, can't I get just a little case of the flu so I don't have to go?

Monday Evening

In the warm dusk we stroll through The Children's Park—an oasis of beauty and caring in the earthquake devastated center of Managua. Playground equipment, much of it built with logs, is freshly painted in many bright colors. There are curving paths and tidy lawns and plantings. Everything is in good repair. Parents push laughing children on the swings.

A lovely little children's library is covered with murals. In one, children hold hands around the world with the words "love" and "peace" written above them. In another, they are breaking the chains of ignorance and reading stacks of colorful books.

Sadly, the park is dedicated to a nine-year-old boy who was executed by Somoza's National Guard for making speeches against the Somoza regime.

As we say grace before dinner back at our hotel, I find myself adding to my normal prayer "...and please let it make me sick so I don't have to go to the war zone!" Instantly I am ashamed and cancel the prayer. Can you do that? Cancel a prayer, I mean. I carefully leave my salad uneaten so I *won't* get sick.

While we eat, we watch the end of a movie from Russia. It is too late to catch what it was about - something romantic, I think. Then there is a public service announcement about not using too many electric cords in one outlet and showing the danger of fire. Many people are just getting electricity for the first time and have to be taught how to use it. On the way home I noticed streetlights in most places.

An American nun has joined our group. Her name is Mary Catherine and she plans to stay here for three years and work. She has intended to come to Central America ever since the four nuns were killed by Death

Squads in El Salvador. Death Squads are an unofficial arm of the U.S. supported dictatorship in that country.

As we change our clothes for our evening meeting, Leticia tells me, "The last time I was here, right after the Revolution, I saw the names of the tortured and the torturers from my home town on a list. When you see names of people you know and went to school with it just..."

She closes her fist against her chest.

"I suppose knowing that one of your old friends was a torturer would be even worse than finding out he'd been tortured," I say.

"Yes, but you know people get into things like that where they forget what is right and wrong because the system seems to force them to do it. They get a job and then they forget that others are human, too. One friend of mine came to the U.S. after the Revolution. He had been a friend of Somoza's so then he had nothing, though he used to be a rich man. I helped him fill out papers for aid and when he told me what he used to earn, I couldn't believe it. He was vice president of this company, and president of that one. He was drawing four full salaries and showing up maybe one day a week at each job."

On the way to our next meeting, we pass through an area of nice stores. Green light bulbs strung across the street spell out the words: *Sandino lives, struggle for peace.* This week is Sandino's birthday. It is fifty years since Somoza had him killed.

Chapter Six

The Miskitu Indian Question

We go to the house of Methodist missionary, Howard Heiner, who is a professional forester now away working as a technical advisor. We've come to meet with The Rev. Norman Bent, a Moravian pastor and leader of the Miskitu Indians. He is himself half Miskitu and has been working very hard to effect a reconciliation between his people and the Sandinista government.

He is a big man, powerfully built, but with an air of gentleness. He speaks English with a lilting West Indies accent:

"In 1982, four thousand, seven hundred, sixty-two Miskitu Indians were evacuated from the area near the Honduran border. A helicopter carrying 75 children crashed in this evacuation which was necessitated by the Contra attacks. Right now, these Indians live in barracks constructed originally for farm workers. New homes are being built for them..."[By the young Germans?]...and they are moving to land of their own. There are about 120,000 Miskitu people in Nicaragua, living mostly on the Atlantic Coast.

"In order for you to understand the problems we have had, it is important for you to understand the background. The east coast of Central America belonged to the British until the 1890's. At that time the land was turned over to the tribes and to groups of Black ex-slaves. There was no integration with the west coast. Even now there is only one road from east to west and that took fifty years to build because of the jungle. The road was finished in 1970 and most of the jungle is still unmapped. In the last 20 years of the Somoza regime, he established two schools on the east coast. Before that the only schools were those built by missionaries.

"For 70 years U.S., Canadian, and Japanese companies exploited the Miskitu Indians in the copper mines. When the mines were nationalized in 1979, all the technicians left, though they were offered the same salaries by the Sandinistas. These mines now produce only 27% of what they once did. There are no parts available for the machines and there is constant harassment by the Contra. Nicaragua is at a disadvantage because it does not have enough Air Force or Coast Guard to protect her rich east coast fishing banks from Honduran fishing.

"The future of Nicaragua is very much tied to this Atlantic Coast which is rich in resources. For years the U.S. companies took wealth out of this area and left nothing. They destroyed the forests and left not even a bridge behind. Now the strategy of the Contra is to destroy the economic base of the country. The Sandinistas are trying to do reforestation in the east but the Contra set forest fires and kill workers with mines and bullets. Let us remember that the Bay of Pigs invasion took place out of eastern Nicaragua. The infrastructure is still there. Reagan showed to the nation a satellite picture of a base which was built for this invasion by the CIA and he called it a Russian missile base."

We all laugh at this, but I don't think anyone thinks it's very funny.

"Well, I happened to be in Puerto Cabezas in March and he spoke in April. When some people described to me that picture, I said that when I was in Puerto Cabezas there were just two airplanes there, besides the one I came on; a 'push-pull' we call it, with two engines, one front and one back and two wings. It is American made..."

"I think it is a Cessna," Mike interjects.

"A Cessna, yes. The Nicaraguan Air Force has put two rockets on it and uses it to protect the coast. There was also the Beechcraft that Commandante William Ramirez, governor of the East Coast, has for his use. Besides this, there are several anti-aircraft guns, but I didn't see any missiles.

"Eastern Nicaragua is very important for a future approach for any possible invasion of Nicaragua from the U.S. Because the infrastructure is still there [from the Bay of Pigs Invasion] the Contra struggles continually to control this area in order to mount an invasion of the rest of the country and establish a provisional government. The O.A.S. would then recognize them. They have been working on this for years now."

He paused and took a deep breath.

"Remember that the Revolution did not take place in the East. For the Indians their country is each little village. In other words, their identity with the land is life to them. The Sandinistas have been trying to integrate the Miskitu people and that's where mistakes were made. Somoza made no mistakes because he abandoned the Indians except to give mining rights to his friends who took out all the gold. I saw it as a boy, in big gold blocks, not just one but many. I saw it with my eyes. They took the gold and left nothing for the people. United Fruit took millions and millions of pounds of bananas out of Puerto Cabezas, but not even running water was left for the city of Puerto Cabezas. Since the Revolution is the first time that the city of Puerto Cabezas has running water. The city now has its main street paved. We even have a sema-phore now. So that was the reality under which the East Coast lived during Somoza. It was total abandonment.

"The Sandinistas, trying to correct this, went in and made several mistakes. The first one was cultural indif-ference. In the East, we have a British culture; in the West a Spanish culture. The East is Protestant: The West, Catholic. A government official even made the terrible mistake of saying we worship a different god. Later he apologized.

"The second mistake was inexperienced leadership. Young kids were sent and tried to do the Revolution too fast. Now the Sandinistas recognize this mistake. The Indians had no concept of nationalism. And there were Nicaraguans living in the West, here, who even thought you had to have a passport to go to the East. They would ask, 'what currency is used over there? I was on a radio talk show the other day and the announcer introduced me saying, 'we have a Nicaraguan brother here,' That is the first time I have heard that, in the old days he would have called me 'a little brownie.'

General laughter follows. The idea of this big man being called a 'little' anything is pretty ludicrous.

"So, after this situation of abandonment of the East by Somoza, the Sandinista decided to take the Revolution to the East for the mutual social and economic benefit. In pursuing this idea, the government made many mistakes. The first mistake was in not recognizing cultural differences. The East Coast is Protestant because the Moravian missionaries came at the invitation of the British Crown; these were German missionaries who came from Jamaica.

"The second mistake was to undermine the authentic local leadership of the people. There was an Indian organization that got started in the late1960's. Somoza repressed it but it survived. This organization had its leadership. They were three university students. One was a young woman, daughter of a store owner, another was a young man who had a Baptist scholarship, and the third was Steadman Fagoth who was secretly given a scholarship from Somoza's security system. Steadman had to give an exchange for his scholarship. He played a double agent role. At the university, he became a very active Sandinista, but he also worked for Somoza. He was able to report–give names. When the others were arrested, he was always arrested, too, but taken to another prison.

"After the Revolution, Steadman Fagoth accused the authentic leadership of the Indian people of being Somosistas [supporters of the deposed dictator]. Because he had been an active Sandinista, [apparently] the Revolution respected him. He was placed at the top and even became the Indian representative in the Council of State."

I glanced around the room. Everyone was writing furiously in their notebooks trying to catch the intricacies of the story.

"Using his position of power, he began to tell the Indian people that they should become an autonomous Indian state. Then the Sandinistas began to investigate and learned of his double agent role. The mistake was made to arrest him without consulting the people. They also arrested some other leaders and that is when the incident occurred in which some people were killed at a church. Eight people were killed, four civilian and four military. The fishing fleet, the mining, the agriculture all stopped and the East became a chaos. People took over churches in protest against Steadman's arrest. That is when the soldiers pushed people out of churches and some fled to Honduras.

"The Sandinistas decided to give Steadman a second chance. He went to the East saying he would support the Sandinista government, but instead he went to Honduras and proclaimed himself an enemy of the Revolution. He went on the radio and asked the Indians to come to Honduras. From there, those who went were financed and trained by the CIA.

"Because of the attacks by these groups, the Sandinistas moved against the Indians. The Contra told the Indians that the Sandinistas were going to put them in concentration camps and burn them and then give their land to Cubans and Vietnamese. Some Indians believed it and they joined the Contra. When the

Moravian Church took a position between the Indian people and the government, the Sandinistas listened. We told them they must release the prisoners. Now there are only eight Miskitu prisoners in all Nicaragua. Tomas Borge said 'we drove the Indians into the hands of the CIA. We are victims of our own mistakes.' But now they are trying very hard to correct this.

"Last week 7 Indians were killed by Contra –innocent people, old people and children. A brand new Moravian church, dedicated just a week before, was bombed by CIA bombs. These people are being destroyed. Who has violated more rights– the Nicaraguan government or the U.S. government?

He paused and cleared his throat.

"Not only is the Sandinista government trying to uplift the Indian culture today, but also there is bilingual education there now. The U.S. is using the Indians. They never knew or cared about us before. The U.S. didn't love its own Indians, so how can they love Indians in Nicaragua?

Although he posed the question gently and without bitterness, I felt a chill. What can we say? He's right.

"No matter what government comes into power, the Indians will still be a minority. It is better for us to make peace with this government where we have already made a start. We now give our young men a conscientious objector letter because we are a historic peace church. The Sandinista government respects this. Only a handful of Contra are fighting for an ideal. The rest are fighting only for money. If you stop the money, you will stop the fighting. We have made many achievements in peacemaking with the Sandinistas. We now have a human rights office in Puerto Cabezas.

"The mistake the Bishops [he means Catholic Bishops] have made here is that they are making propaganda out of their disagreement. Their last pastoral letter was even released abroad before it was released here. If they had gone quietly to the Junta like we did, those kids [the Junta?] would have listened. We go to the Sandinistas so angry we almost have a fist fight but we have quiet diplomacy and end up hugging each other by the end of the meeting."

This man appears to have great intelligence and integrity. He reminds me of Dave with a dark tan.

"Please bear in mind that this country is not a Communist country. It is not. But there is no way Nicaragua can be stopped from being a socialist country.

We take turns posing for pictures with this kindly, patient man, and then file back onto the bus (which now feels like home) and go back to the hotel through quiet, tree-lined streets.

Major Fact for today: what Reagan said about the missile bases was not true. I am surprised that I can still feel such disappointment over the lack of veracity of elected officials. I had thought my disillusion was complete and total on the day when Good Old Ike said, "No, it wasn't a weather plane after all, it was a U2 spy plane." If Ike could lie then who could be trusted? But I still trust anyhow, even though I know better.

Before going to sleep, I look at Dave's picture on my bedside table. Being away from him is still like an amputation. My loneliness refreshed, I pull the sheet up to my neck. Leticia's voice from the other bed says, "good night; sleep tight."

My mother used to say that.

Chapter Seven

From Catholic to Protestant and Back Again

Tuesday morning

Early morning sounds: our fan, the air conditioner next door, and a radio (or tape?) in the room next to us playing a Strauss waltz. It is cloudy and cool, very pleasant for eating breakfast in the breezeway. A light wind is blowing through the iron gate that serves as a front door for the hotel.

I skim through the newspaper that someone has left on the table – *La Barricada,* the Sandinista paper. An ad exhorts the people to vote in the upcoming elections. "We are free and we will have a right to choose," it says. This morning we will be going to talk to Bishop Vega. He is president of the Council of Bishops and is, therefore, the highest ranking Catholic prelate in the country. Although we only usually hear about Vega and Oblando y Bravo, there are actually nine Catholic Bishops in Nicaragua.

An Interview With Bishop Vega

Our bus pulls up in front of a new and very luxurious office building. Clearly, this is not someone's recycled home! The ceilings are all made up of intricate tropical wood paneling. The floors are gorgeous white tile; the walls are gleaming white. Is this how God's office looks in Heaven? We are led down wide hallways past glassed-in courtyards.

It is interesting to note that the government has not touched church property here. After the Mexican Revolution, much Church property was confiscated.

Bishop Vega is a short, round man. His face crinkles up into genial rolls of gleaming brown skin. He is dressed all in white clerical garb. We are all directed to sit around a large table. He seats himself at the head of the table and states that he wishes to have a dialogue.

A blunt question from someone behind me begins the discussion. "Which would you choose, socialism or capitalism?"

The Bishop smiles, "We must have some kind of socialism because the people in this society–the workers– have been marginalized. But there is a great difference between the socialism that comes from totalitarian countries and is only materialistic, and the socialism that is needed here. Almost the only problem we have with the government is that they are totalitarian and materialistic. We have a real dialectic position with this so that no man or no class can be over another in order to dominate it."

At this point, a servant woman enters carrying a glass of ice water on a glass plate. The water glass is topped by another glass plate. She places it by the Bishop's left hand. He does not acknowledge her presence, but continues to speak.

"They [the Sandinistas, I assume] think that everything is finished, everything is perfect, and everything coming from outside is 'Contra.'" He lifts the plate carefully from the top of the glass, sips some water, then replaces the plate.

Another question: "How can dialogue be possible when you won't say Mass for the dead Sandinistas?"

I sensed, more than saw, a slight pout cross the Bishop's round face.

"This is not true. Sometimes there are particular cases and then the Sandinistas try to manipulate and cry and convert the people. Sometimes they try to force the people to say what they want. We try to have some agreements about 'why don't you give us our mail without opening it first?' and they say 'well, we cannot.' A man who was arrested was said to have had a heart attack in prison, but when the family opened the coffin they found he had been beaten."

I fueled up my courage, cleared my throat and asked a question of my own. "Sir, I respect your attempts at constructing a dialectic and find it a very hopeful sign. I share your concern for human rights and I am terribly concerned about the atrocities committed by the Contra. They have tortured and killed helpless old people and children. One of our Methodist missionaries wrote and told us of a twenty-two year old health worker who was beheaded by the Contra. Given all these incidents, could the Bishops issue a condemnation of Contra excesses as well as Sandinista excesses?"

"There have been many excesses. The Contra have a desire for revenge. You have to remember they are very angry at the Sandinistas."

I found myself plowing on with uncharacteristic tenacity. "I'm sorry," I said, "I'm trying to understand. It seems you are saying that it is normal for the Contra to want revenge on the Sandinistas, but not for some Sandinistas to have a need for revenge after 40 years of brutality suffered at the hands of the National Guard who are now the Contra. I'm sorry. Maybe I don't understand the reasoning."

Bishop Vega smiled. The corners of his eyes crinkled. He lifted the glass plate and took another sip of ice water.

"Yes, you don't understand because the situation here is not understandable. It is not available to reason. When a people fight against each other it is not a reasonable thing."

Still smiling, the Bishop turned to the next questioner.

"But would it not be better if the U.S. did not use these Contra for their own purposes?"

"Yes, it would be better if all other countries stayed out, Cuba and Russia also. I said the other day to Mr. Stone [the president's special advisor on Latin America] 'You speak like protectors and not neighbors. That is not right for these times. That is a very poor language for these times.'"

Bill raises a tentative hand. "Do you use a process of wide consultation when you write your pastoral letters? What is the process? Who are the theologians with whom you consult?"

"We are constantly in consultation in my diocese. I don't know about the others. Some others have not had the same contact with the people. Since Medallen, we are more in the life of the people. There is more communicative spirit. It surprises me sometimes how people from the States think they have all the answers. Here we are at the moment where the Church is trying to promote the spiritual development. The Jesuits come and they have not the idea of how a small group in Latin America guides the people. Jesuits think like liberals."

Funny how "liberal" has become a bad word. Doesn't it mean "generous"? I think that's what the dictionary says.

"We are always going to do this for the poor, but they do not think with the poor. They have this mentality that the poor must always be treated like the poor and not like ourselves. I am not working with the marginal people. I passed my childhood in El Salvador and when I came back, I had no idea of the conditions here. But I see how the priests prepare the plans for the people and not do the plan with them. The North Americans have the idea to do everything in a certain time, like 'we will do this in two years,' but you don't come in with precepts. We need to stay with the people and to see what they want; what are their necessities? Not just put like a straight jacket on them. The problem for the Church is to promote how to be responsible and free men. You don't realize this because you have had from the beginning the opportunity to be equal..."

This is all very nice, but what does it have to do with the question? I would mention this out loud but I don't want to be one of those Yankees who "has all the answers."

The Bishop continues, "...must rescue for the people their own image. Some leaders of the Church are with the elite and do not really represent the people. It is said that the Church is divided but what we are doing is to promote a new understanding that will awake the people. But the popular Church is not this. The popular Church is through the struggle of the classes to destroy one another, to say they have the right even to kill the other class..."

Hasn't the Church always told people they have the right, or duty, to kill during wartime?

"... I do not say the popular Church is really a division coming from the Church, but a strategy to divide the Church. Political liberation is not enough, we must rescue the human quality of everyone."

The questions are coming quick and fast, now.

"Don't you feel that the Sandinista government pays more attention to human rights than the National Guard did?"

"They build schools and health facilities, but they have not attended to human development. That is why we are always trying to put the human element in the Revolution, but we are not in the spirit of the Contra." [Didn't answer the question again.]

Another question: "Don't you think that the literacy campaign helps to develop the people?"

"If I set before you a very good dinner, it looks good and smells good but it is poison..."

"Oh, I see. You are saying there is a literacy campaign so that they can read Marx."

"Yes, so it is always this hate put in people."

The Bishop's secretary stands in the doorway. He rises, signaling that the interview is concluded. We gather cameras and tape recorders and rise too. On the way out he smiles and nods and shakes hands with everyone.

On our way to the next appointment, we stop at the new municipal marketplace. It is huge, block after block of corrugated iron stalls all painted orange and very clean. Leticia marvels at the cleanliness.

"Before the Revolution this place was filthy," she says as we walk between rows of hanging dresses, "The people were filthy, too. They had no pride. Their clothes were always dirty and you'd see them sitting right in the middle of dirty, running water. Now look how clean their clothes are!"

I've noticed that even in the poorest neighborhoods the children are clean and nicely dressed. That's a real contrast with Peru and Bolivia. Many of the stalls in the market are filled with children's clothes. Brightly colored paperback children's books dominate the bookseller's stall. A cursory examination shows no Marxist messages; only colors, shapes, counting, and bits of poetry.

AT THE HEADQUARTERS OF CEPAD: THE PROTESTANT ORGANIZATION

Back in the bus and across town, we stop in a crowded neighborhood of one and two story buildings. The lower floors are mostly shops, the upper floors, most with balconies, appear to be residences. We cross the street and are directed to a two story wooden structure. It is distinguished from the others on the street by the armed guard who stands in front of the gate and by the barbed wire that tops the wooden wall.

We are led up a narrow outside staircase, across the second story veranda, and down a dark hall. Just as I am about to feel a bit claustrophobic, a smiling young woman shows us into a conference room in which a sumptuous lunch has been set out. We are greeted by Dr. Sixto Ulba and, after a prayer; we all sit down to lunch. Dr. Ulba speaks:

"First I want to thank you for visiting us at this very critical time in our history. Yesterday I had a meeting with 48 pastors. Last week I had a meeting with 42 pastors on the border of Honduras. This is because the Bishops' letter had a very negative effect even on Protestants. I asked these pastors who were all from rural areas if there was religious persecution in their areas. I asked, 'are children of your congregations studying Marxism in school?' They said none of these things are occurring."

"There is a problem of food distribution in this country. If you come back in a few months, you will not have the food like we are having today. There is a blockade by the U.S. so we cannot get medicines. We are in a situation of war. When I went up to the border, I saw no one else on the road the last 45 km. I was scared. As I came around a bend in the road, I saw people on horses. I was even more scared. I thought what would I do if they were Contra? The Contra are doing a lot of banditry within the country, so it is very human to be afraid."

Thank you! That makes me feel better about my own fears of this coming weekend. "...only human to be afraid."

"The pastors in one region told me that 27 of their youth have been killed in the period from January to May of this year and this is only in one small area. These youths were from 12 to 19 years of age. At least 3 times each day U.S. planes fly over this region."

He goes to the map and points (uh oh!) to Ocotal. He returns to his seat looking tired and grim.

"There are 1,500 Protestant pastors in Nicaragua. We are 15% of the total population. We are talking now about direct aid to church members whose farms and homes have been destroyed by Contra and whose family members have been raped and killed. I am a member of the Committee for Human Rights here in Nicaragua. it is very important for you to be aware if there is any religious persecution here. We have a Protestant radio station. We can invite any of you to preach in any church. Decide for yourselves if that is persecution. We have had problems–serious problems. There was one time when mobs did occupy some churches. There was a time when there were problems with the Mormons and Jehovah's Witnesses. There are some problems between church and government but we can sit down together and talk it over. We criticize the mob takeovers and the problems with the Miskitus.

"There still are problems with the Jehovah's Witnesses. The problem is that the Jehovah's Witnesses do not recognize the state and won't take part in political activities. The people here thought that meant that they were against the Revolution. People began to believe that all Protestants were like that because they did not understand that there are differences between denominations. Two churches were taken over by mobs but were returned within 24 hours.

"There were only 12 Jewish families in Nicaragua and they were all sympathetic to Somoza. Most left after the Revolution abandoning the Synagogue which was then taken over by the government. Recently they were asked if they wanted it back. They said they couldn't afford to keep it open and besides they had no rabbi. The problem is that the Sandinista Children's Organization now has a headquarters there and so Jews who come here to visit take pictures of the Synagogue with slogans and posters all over the outside of it. We have recommended that the government move the Children's Organization. We took a group of Jews from New York to see the Synagogue recently and I told them they could take it over right away if they wanted to, but they didn't want to.

"One message you should be taking back is that this government has the political will to sit down and discuss peace with anyone. Reagan is the one who has been promoting the war here. I attended the meeting with the Kissinger Commission. What I saw was the power of the Empire. We sat down and they asked questions like 'was it true that women were raped in prisons and priests killed?' and other ridiculous question like that. When it was our turn to make a statement, do you know what Kissenger said? He said, 'our time is up now.'"

The Kissenger Commission spent only 8 hours in the country and they spent most of that time with the opposition speakers who were brought into the Embassy.

Dr. Ulba continues, "The day I have information that the government is torturing people in prison, I will be the first to denounce them. One day a man came to me and said a soldier had hit him. They'd hitched a ride into town together and gotten into an argument, which led to a fight. I went with this man to the FMLN and that soldier was sentenced to 8 months in prison.

"We believe as Christians that we have to do prophetic work in this country. We do not intend to be just another group of Sandinistas. In March, a drunk army officer ran over several people who were in a religious procession. The officer was stripped of his military stripes and shirt and given a prisoner's shirt. He was sentenced to 30 years."

A lady brings coffee in to us. Dr. Ulba is served in turn. He smiles and thanks her, then thanks us all for coming.

Tuesday Afternoon - Fernando Cardenal, Director of CDS

The bus deposits us across the street from the Ministry of Culture. We trudge across a little bridge towards the Ministry's oasis of trees. On the far side of the bridge is an opening in the cyclone fence that surrounds the grounds. There is no gate or guard. Under the trees a soft breeze is blowing. Mike indicates we are to sit on folding chairs, which have been arranged in a circle on a stone paved patio. Above us, arch the branches of a fig tree large enough to shelter an entire city block.

Mike disappears into the one story, brick building and emerges in a moment with a tall, athletic looking man, youthful in appearance despite his silver hair. He introduces him as Fernando Cardenal, a Jesuit priest like his brother, poet Ernesto Cardenal. His face, though obviously bearing signs of fatigue, is kindly and intelligent.

"It is very important for us that people like you come to Nicaragua to see the truth about our country," he says, speaking in Spanish as Mike translates. "After meeting with you, I will meet with five women lawyers from the U.S. Yesterday I spoke with European reporters. I think that little by little we can change the disinformation about us. I would like to thank you for coming to Nicaragua. Rather than give a speech, I think it would be best for us just to talk."

Mike says, "Could you start out by telling us what it is that you do?"

"Yes, of course. After the Triumph, I was given the responsibility of organizing the Literacy Campaign. Now I am the director of the CDS, or Block Committees. (In July, Fr. Cardenal was named Minister of Education.)

Debby asks, "We met with Bishop Vega this morning. He says that the Literacy Campaign was like giving poisoned food to the people. He says you are promoting Marxism and class war; that you promote hate."

Father Cardenal nods sadly. Clearly, he's heard this many times before. "The materials are available for you to read. Examine them and see for yourselves if you think they are poison. This is an example of the kind of charges they make, but I can prove to you that it is false."

Question: "What about the charge that the Block Committees are just a way of controlling the people?"

If Father Cardenal took this pointed query as an attack, he showed no sign. His tone, as he replied, was respectful of both question and questioner.

"The C.D.S. has many roles to carry out. We're in charge of the health projects and, by the way, Nicaragua is the only Latin American country that has not had any cases of polio in the past two years. We are promoting a food project encouraging everyone to have a vegetable garden in whatever little space they have. We are teaching people to build little stoves that can use any kind of garbage for fuel.

"It is necessary to unite neighborhoods to meet their needs for electricity and water. It is also important to control the price of food so there are not shortages. Our block committees have controlled crime, so there is vigilance, but to say that they are to control people is a caricature. Participation is entirely voluntary. It is often charged that we control food, but we do not control food supplies, we control food prices.

"In each block, those who want to participate in C.D.S. meet and elect officers democratically. The coordinators from many C.D.S. groups in the neighborhood meet for a coordinating committee. All of these committees in a zone elect one representative to coordinate for a region and then, at the national level, we give services to regional coordinators. But the block committee is the base. People who do not participate in C.D.S. have no political problems. In my block we don't even have a C.D.S. and nothing bad happens to us as a result."

Question: "Why are we seeing so many Marxist books in the bookstores? That seems to substantiate what Bishop Vega says."

"Marxism is a very difficult science. I was a philosophy professor at the university and I know how difficult it is to understand. Anyone who has just finished learning to read and write is not going to be able to understand a book on Marxism. Now I'm not saying we don't read Marx here. You can read anything you want here. I'm just saying the literacy campaign is not for the purpose of teaching the people to study Marxism. To go from there to say we promote hate...well, if we had wanted to promote hate we would have had firing squads after the Revolution, we did not. Christ says, 'Know them by their fruits.' If you see Marxist poison in our materials then you will know I have been lying."

Leticia said, "My nursemaid who is living in Nicaragua...and looking at me you can tell how old she must be... sent a letter to me at my home in San Francisco. She had a very lovely message in it and she told me so proudly, 'I have just learned to write.'"

The fatigue seemed to drop from Father Cardenal's face and he smiled with genuine joy.

"That has always been a great thrill for me, to receive letters like the one you speak of. During the Literacy Campaign I received a great many letters from people, many of whom had just learned to read and write after a lifetime of being illiterate. I kept these letters pinned to the wall and reread them often."

The stones on the patio radiated stored up late spring heat, but questions continued: "Is Nicaragua a Marxist state?"

"Marxism is not a political system, it is a method of analysis. The fact that one studies Marxism does not mean that one has formed an alliance with the U.S.S.R. I am a Jesuit priest. When I studied to be a priest, I studied Marxism because it is important to understand it. For us Marxism is not a problem that is discussed in the same way as in the U.S. The U.S. has a political problem with another country so persons who live in either country are profoundly agitated by that problem.

"Here, our problems are misery, poverty, and the attack by the U.S. The U.S.S.R. has never attacked us. The U.S. has occupied and dominated our country for 150 years–that is the imperialism we know. The imperialism of the U.S.S.R. is not a problem to us. The reason why Reagan says we are a danger to the U.S. is to get money from Congress to fight us. But we are not a satellite to anyone and don't wish to be. If we wanted to be a satellite, it would have been better to remain a satellite of the U.S.!"

Question:" What are the relations now between the Nicaraguan government and the free enterprise sector of the economy? How do they feel about price controls?"

"Here, in Nicaragua, we have a mixed economy sixty percent of which is in private hands. Right now we have a serious food shortage and so there is a problem of elevated prices. Between the food producers and the consumers are a series of merchants. Each raises the price of a commodity. So, what we are trying to do is to encourage people to grow more of their own food. For eight vital products, we will try to eliminate the middleman so that the consumer can have the food at production cost. The rich in Nicaragua have lost some of their importance. In the past the poor were treated like trash, now they are the important ones. Some of the rich don't like this and if they don't..." he smiles, "they go to Miami."

A soft breeze is stirring the fig leaves in lazy circles above us. Some insects with voices like cicadas, only much louder, add their own touch of 'elevator' music.

Question: "What will happen to all these middle men? Won't they be unemployed?"

Father Cardenal nods, acknowledging the importance of the question, "There is plenty of work in this country. We need teachers. They can do the kind of work that we need, not make money on food that should go to the poor."

Ah, now here is a fact that is open to a variety of interpretations. To many people in the U.S. this is going to sound like a totalitarian statement. Sounds like a limitation on personal freedom. The trouble is which freedom is more important? The freedom of a few people to make a lot of money in pursuing their chosen careers, or the freedom of the majority of people to have food at affordable prices. Not a simple question. Finding Facts is unlikely to help resolve this point.

Question: "We understand the Pope has ordered you to quit your government post. Do you intend to obey this order?"

As he hears the question translated, a hint of pain touches his face.

"I want to do what I believe is God's will. It would be very easy for me to quit. I am a priest. If I quit the government, my future and my old age would be guaranteed. To stay in this Revolution is only danger. I drive around Managua with no bodyguard. I could be killed any day. But I believe that Christ wants me to follow the parable of the Good Shepherd. If I abandon my people now I am like the Levite who passes by on the other side."

He makes these statements without self-dramatization, just matter-of-factly, but with dedication so intense that there is the impression that his conscience never admitted the possibility of choice.

He continues, "The human being is more than just a commercial being. The drugs and punk movement in some countries are because the youth have no larger goals. When I was in West Germany, I saw graffiti written on a wall that said 'there is no future.' But the West Germany youth have everything. Their summer cottages are like the homes of the rich in Nicaragua. When I saw that graffiti I thought that the youth in our country would say, 'there is a great future–to rebuild our country!'

"You see, you don't feel good by sniffing chemicals, but by building something. When I went to a conference in San Francisco, I visited my sister who lives there. She said to me 'why don't you stay here where everything is beautiful?' I didn't answer her because I knew she could not understand. It is nice to have lots of everything like in the U.S., but it is much better to be here where we lack so much. The human renewal that is taking place here is a greater joy."

As he speaks, his face seems lit from within by the reflection of images we can only vaguely imagine.

"In my college teaching I tried to teach my students the value of unselfish service, I achieved that very rarely. But now I see that the Revolution is teaching this to youth. The Revolution is a school. Nicaragua is one of the richest countries in the world because it has a youth that is worth treasures. I have another sister who lives here. She does not understand the Revolution, but what can I do? Everyone is free. She is entitled to her opinion.

Father Cardenal continues to speak about his brother, Ernesto, about the visit of the Pope to Nicaragua, and about the work of the Block Committees. When he tells of the attacks by the Contras, a deep sadness and frustration seems to overtake him, but still there is no hint of anger. He says, "You should not sleep comfortably as long as your country uses your money to kill our women and children. You have to do something!"

The lady lawyers are crossing the bridge and ducking diffidently under the branches of the fig tree. Father Cardenal rises and we echo the motion. He suggests a prayer and we all catch hands in a circle. He says perhaps one of our pastors might lead the prayer. Mike does this. After the concluding "Amen," Fernando Cardenal walks around the circle shaking hands with each of us in turn and saying a few personal words of thanks and farewell. Then, without a break, he begins his meeting with the lawyers.

Cardenal and Vega. Two men – two opposing positions. As the rest of the group tours the Ministry of Culture Museum, I sit alone in a tiled courtyard trying to hold both men in my mind. I turn them this way and that, as if by juxtaposition I could weigh their souls.

I was impressed by Bishop Vega, a man of cherubic charm, but Father Cardenal has something more. With him there is the unmistakable sense of being in the presence of a good and humble man, a man who can love the poor individually as well as collectively.

The fact is that the example of Fernando Cardenal is so powerful that as we say grace before dinner that night, I find myself unexpectedly praying for strength, not illness. I am ready to go to Ocotal and take my chances with the Contra.

Tuesday Evening

Back on the bus and down curving streets. Tree branches thump the metal sides and we stop in front of a house that would have looked quite at home in Bel Air. This is the house once occupied by the head of Somoza's (Civil) Aviation Service, the man who ordered the bombing of civilian populations during the weeks before the Triumph. When Somoza left, he did too, and now his house is occupied by one of the Solentiname artists, a peasant woman named Olivia, and her large extended family. Like others who gave special service to the Revolution, she was awarded one of the many abandoned mansions in Managua.

Although she had no formal training, Olivia's paintings are now exhibited in galleries around the world. Despite the fact that she has become an international celebrity, Olivia meets us at the door and escorts us inside as unpretentiously as if she were still back in the islands of Solentiname. She is a tiny lady and appears to be what Victorian writers were fond of referring to as "careworn".

[Some background here: The island group collectively known as "Solentiname" is in the southern part of Lake Nicaragua. The islands are lush, tropical and beautiful, but the inhabitants were very poor. Then, in 1965, Ernesto Cardenal, Trappist Monk, poet, and brother of Fernando, came to the islands and established a religious community where he encouraged the artistic expression of the people. He also facilitated discussion groups around study of the Gospel and social justice. Subsequently, many islanders joined the Revolution and, as a result, Somoza's National Guard killed many of them and burned their villages to the ground.]

Inside the house, the lights are dim. Our footsteps sound hollow on the lovely white tiles. The rooms, though spacious, are innocent of furniture except for a few chairs and many easels on which are suspended some of the famous Solentiname paintings. Done in a faintly Grandma Moses style (known by artists as "primitive"), these paintings tell stories from the life of Jesus as if he were a Nicaraguan peasant. The settings are lush and tropical; the people are life-like if somewhat one-dimensional. More paintings hang on the walls and are propped on the back of the single sofa.

We move into a room (which I am discovering every large Nicaraguan house has) that is open to the breezes. These rooms are usually in the middle of the houses rather than at one end like a porch, and thus channel fresh air through the center of the dwelling. As we seat ourselves on chairs and on the floor, we are aware of children's voices coming from a kind of family room area raised about six steps above us. Mothers and children seem to be watching television up there. Occasionally a baby cries. The house smells of food past its prime.

Olivia sits in a rocker. In the dim light her voice, firm and confident, seems to be coming from a body much larger than the frail tiny one that we can see.

"We have had a rebirth in our spiritual life because of Ernesto Cardenal," she says, "He discovered a group of islands, our islands, where religion had been poorly taught. It was like an opium to make people conform to the evils of life. By reading and discussion the Gospels together, we discovered their meaning. Through the dialogue over the Gospels we started asking, 'is there injustice in the world? Where does it come from?' Little by little, we thought of ways to change it. Now we no longer think of just our small community, but all of Nicaragua. Before the Revolution there were no day care centers or health centers or cooperatives for the people. There were only things for a very few.

"When Ernesto Cardenal came to the islands he saw what misery we lived in and he thought that was not just [as in "Justice"]. Solentiname was such an abandoned place we did not have a school so we continued to be ignorant. He brought us paints and taught us how to paint pictures. He would bring the paintings to Managua and sell them then bring the money back to the community.

"I used to be one of the most traditional of the Catholics and I said that we had to wait until we died for happiness. Now I believe that religion and revolution are the same thing. Four of my sons and two of my daughters fought in the Revolution."

She motions toward a beautiful girl with long dark hair who sits on the steps to the family room. The girl appears to be in her early twenties. She rewards our attention with a shy smile.

"You see," Olivia continues, "we had to be willing to give our lives for others. Even Christ gave his life for others. The words of the Gospel give courage. Fear is natural..."

Who else said that? Oh yes, Sixto Ulba.

"...but you have to overcome the fear. Jesus said that those who try to keep their lives will loose them, but those who are willing to give up their lives shall gain them."

A question comes out of the dimness of the room: "Why do you think the U.S. sees Nicaragua as such a threat?"

"I think it is because the U.S. is used to manipulating poor people. They took the gold out of Nicaragua and left nothing. The rich people in Nicaragua are uncomfortable now because they no longer have the special privileges they used to have so it is useful for the U.S. to use these people to attack the Revolution."

Question: "What happened to the Solentiname community?"

"Ernesto Cardenal helped us to learn a skill. Somoza said that was Communism. The National Guard destroyed our village. They tortured people."

Her voice becomes hoarse as she begins to speak of her son. His picture is on the wall. He looks to have been about 15. She turns her face away.

The daughter continues the story. "We, that is the young people, knew we had to do something as the pressure on us increased. Our community was pacifist so we knew we would have to go against their teachings. We saw that we were going to be killed anyway so we might as well do something with our deaths. We prepared an attack on the National Guard San Carlos Arsenal. It was after that attack that my brother was killed. He did not die in the attack; they caught him afterwards in a field and tortured him to death. After the attack on the San Carlos Arsenal, the National Guard destroyed our village. They killed many of our people and the rest were scattered."

Her mother continues. "We know that many of you are aware and do carry out very good work in the U.S., but many people in your country are asleep like opium, and don't even know where Nicaragua is. Reagan uses television to sell anything to the American people. He tells them they must kill 'gorillas'[sic, her emphasis is more apparent in Spanish than it is in this translation] in some countries, and that they must stop Communists in Nicaragua. And the people believe it."

Her daughter adds, "As Christians you can tell your own Christian communities what is really happening here because there is so much disinformation about us. The best thing you can do is to come here and see the freedom that exists and to tell others back home."

Olivia continues, "Jesus says, 'feed the hungry, comfort the sick,' that's what this Revolution is doing. Those Catholic Bishops who speak against us used to receive big boxes of champagne from Somoza, but if a poor person came to their house, he would not have even been allowed to sit down. What kind of religion is that?"

Olivia continues by telling us about how she and other members of her household now teach art to the National Guardsmen who are imprisoned in Managua. Because the only Guardsmen still detained (the others having been pardoned) are serving sentences for war crimes, Olivia knows that these men are the worst of the torturers–possibly even the men who killed her son.

"We now teach art to the men who killed our children," she says, "so they need not continue to behave like animals but should be human beings. In time, they will be reborn as we were."

I would like to say to Bishop Vega, 'is this teaching hate?' I wish I could see him discuss this with her.

Question: "Reagan says that the government of Nicaragua practices terrorism against its own people. Is this true?"

"No. The fighting comes from outside. You can go up to the border and see for yourselves where the terrorism comes from."

Riding home on the bus Leticia tells me about the holes people knocked in the walls of their houses in Matagalpa (her home town) during the Revolution so that the *muchachas* (Sandinistas) could travel the entire length of a block of joined houses without ever going outside. I wonder if the people in the U.S. realize that if we couldn't win in Vietnam where the peasants were highly demoralized, we could never win here where the people have had five years to taste freedom and proudly state their willingness to die to preserve it.

Even if we did succeed in dominating Nicaragua again, it would be a constant struggle to maintain control. Sandino has been dead for 50 years and he is not forgotten. Moreover, if we encourage Honduras to attack Nicaragua, who's to say that Honduras will prevail? I believe that the Nicaraguans would encourage the Honduran peasant soldiers to turn their guns on their superiors and defect. You cannot win a war by sending people with no stake in the system against people who are defending their own freedom.

On the TV news at dinnertime tonight we saw Daniel Ortega and several other members of the ruling Junta on *Cara De Puebla* (Face the Nation.) The site was a technical school and earnest young students were giving speeches about how they would defend their country to the death. Their faces were so sensitive and beautiful, must they really die? How can we prevent it?

Chapter Eight

Elections and Health Care

Wednesday morning

The nun who is with our group spent the night at the house of her order and when she returned to the hotel this morning; she brought two sisters with her. One of the sisters has been in Nicaragua since 1956. I'm anxious to talk with her and elicit Facts.

"What changes have you seen?" I ask, "are things better now than before the Revolution?"

She looks at me as if I were not terribly bright, but answers gently, "Of course things are much better for the poor. That's why the people who were rich are not so happy now."

In the few minutes before the bus comes to pick us up, I sit on the front steps of the hotel thinking about Bishop Vega. Why did he brush off my questions about the Contra atrocities? How could he balance a story about one man suffering a heart attack after being roughed up in jail (something that happens often enough in the U.S., sad to say) against the brutal and systematic murders of thousands of innocent people?

I do respect the Bishop. He seems to be a kindly man, but it is as if he has a large blind spot. He can see only the faults of the Revolution and none of its benefits. On the other hand, he is ready to excuse the Contra from any guilt. I don't recall that he ever quoted Scripture or even mentioned the name of Christ. (A quick check of my notes confirms this). I understand that may be due to a difference of tradition, but it still makes me wonder about his focus.

The Supreme Electoral Council

Our first stop today is at the Supreme Electoral Council. It is housed in a modern office building unguarded by any barbed wire. We are told that our cameras will be opened (to check for bombs, I suppose) so I quickly take my last two pictures and remove the roll of film. No one stops us, however, and we enter the government offices unfrisked and unchecked.

We are to meet with the President of the Council. His is the group that will oversee the November elections. The procedural model for these elections will be that which is used in Costa Rica.

When the President of the Council, Dr. Miriano Fiallo Huanguerre, enters the conference room where we are seated, there is a general scraping back of chairs as we all scramble to stand. He smiles and shakes his head waving, with what looks like embarrassment, for us to sit down.

Dr. Fiallo is a tall, handsome man of middle age, dignified without being officious. As he seats himself at the far end of the table, he asks us with a smile if we would prefer to suffer through his English or would we prefer that he use a translator. He certainly doesn't seem to have anything to apologize for concerning his English. We opt for English:

"Anyone 16 years of age or more, who is not serving a prison term, will be eligible to vote in the elections. We, as in the U.S., do not have a national identification system, so we are setting up 5,000 polling places where citizens can register to vote. This registration will occur at the end of July. We are setting up many so that people will vote in the neighborhoods where they are known. We hope this will prevent double registration and other possible fraud.

"In July each voter will be given a registration card to vote. We are not using computers because when there are only a few people who know how to work them in the country, fraud would be easy.

"When voting occurs the voter will be given two ballots - one for president and vice president and one for a representative. The people will not select persons, but parties. The proportion of the vote will be assigned to each party and representation will be on this basis. Because there will be two ballots, people will be able to vote for one party for president/vice president and a different party for representation."

Through the windows of the conference room, I see that the back fence of the garden is topped by a garnish of barbed wire. A uniformed man, whom I first took to be a guard, seems to be the gardener.

We are training personnel to act as election workers. We are also importing the materials we need to make records, ballot boxes and curtains to keep the voting secret. We want to keep the campaign short because a long campaign would cost too much. We want to have an election in Nicaragua that, for the first time, will be free and honest. Our electoral law is very open. For the registration of candidates we will have probably 10 parties that could register candidates; Social Christian, Liberal Independent, Conservative Democrat, Socialist, F.S.L.N/Sandinista, Social Democrat, popular Action Movement, and Communist. I think it is very important for people in the U.S. to realize that there is a Communist party in Nicaragua and that it is not the Sandinistas! Some of the Communists did join with the Sandinistas before the Revolution, but now they are back to being a separate party."

Question: "What information will be required from people registering to vote?"

"Full name, date of birth, address, sex, and any sort of I.D.: Passport, social security card, or driver's license. If you have no I.D. all you have to do is to have two witnesses verify that they know you."

He goes on to explain that people will need to decide where they are going to vote, either in the area where they live or the area where they work.

"I, for instance, will register here in Managua because it is where I work, although my home is Matagalpa and I would much rather be there!"

He smiles gently with a light touch of self-mockery. He obviously does not take himself too seriously, though he is very serious about his job.

A young woman comes in the room carrying coffee in demitasse cups for everyone. Each saucer holds also two dainty cookies. The serving starts at the end of the table furthest from Dr. Fiallo and he is served in his turn, neither first nor last. Leticia takes this opportunity to lean over and whisper to me that Dr. Fiallo's father was one of her literature professors and that Dr. Fiallo is himself a professor of law at the University in Matagalpa. My impression of the man is that he is intelligent and sincere, probably with a wry sense of humor. My impression of all the government officials I have met so far is that they are honest people.

Questioning resumes: "Will there be absentee ballots?"

"No, this is our first election. We are not so sophisticated that we can do that. Besides most of our absentees are living abroad and we would have no way of controlling for fraud in those cases."

I expect this will be a point by which some will seek to discredit the elections.

Question: "Will there be foreign observers present?"

"In the past we have had foreign controlled elections. In 1927, the president of the Electoral Commission (my job) was a U.S. Marine officer."

This is an accurate statement. I read this also.

"However, we will give as many people as wish to, the freedom to visit polls and report whatever they see."

Question: "How will members of the armed forces register?"

"It will be the same as with everyone; either where they live or where they work. If they can't be in either place then they won't be able to vote."

Question: "Is it true what we hear in the U.S. that the majority of the people are against the Revolution and that the Sandinistas will loose the election?"

"The second part of your question I cannot answer because first, I do not know who will win and to guess would compromise my position as unbiased, you understand. As to the first part of the question, I think the best way for you to answer that is to go out and talk to people, find out how they feel."

As the time allotted to us drew to a close, Dr. Fiallo stood and shook hands with each of us. His parting words were, "We appreciate very much your visit to Nicaragua. We know we are not perfect, but we are working very hard to see that we have a fair election."

On the way back to our hotel for lunch, we stop to do a bit of sightseeing in the Plaza of the Revolution where we saw the militia drill on our first night here. Leticia and I enter the battered old National Palace building and mingle with the government workers on their lunch break. They are friendly and smile and nod as we pass them on the stairs and in the halls. Leticia carries on a long and lively conversation with a young man from a tax office. He seems to be happy with the new government and excited about the possibilities for rebuilding his country.

Wednesday afternoon - Health Care

The bus is late in picking us up after lunch, but it's nice to just sit on the front steps of the hotel and watch the people go by. I feel very much at home in this pleasant, middle-class neighborhood. Schoolgirls in simple cotton blouses and blue jean skirts walk by chatting and giggling. School uniforms are worn everywhere in

Latin America, but in most countries expensive wool uniforms are themselves a barrier to school attendance for the very poor. The profits resulting from the contracts for supply of uniforms provides another opportunity for corruption. This cotton blouse and blue jean solution seems like a good one to me. The kids look neat and comfortable, yet the uniforms are inexpensive, easily obtained, and washable.

A young man with a t-square under his arm hurries toward the bus stop. An occasional late model Japanese car scoots by. The nice thing here is that when you smile at someone on the street, they smile back. Even under attack as they are, the people are open and friendly.

Once more we are using Howard Heiner's house, though I still have not met him. Maria de Zuniga, an American lady about my own age, is speaking to us:

"I came here as a Peace Corps worker under Somoza. Because I was a health care worker, I quickly learned about the corruption in the system. The only programs that had funding were the malaria and birth control programs. Medical workers would have 3 or 4 jobs that they were collecting salaries for (but seldom worked at) plus a private practice. After the Revolution the Sandinista government was faced with this corrupt system and almost no health care in the countryside. Under Somoza, half of all children born died before their first birthday. They died of malnutrition and bad water.

"In July 1979 [days after the Triumph], the Sandinista government created the national health care system. They stated that health care is a right of all the people.

Health care was not socialized, but all health care is free as is medicine. Along with this health care system, the doctors were able to continue private practice, but not to charge exorbitant fees. The doctors were encouraged to stay in the country by allowing them to keep private practice.

"Now there are two major priority areas in government health programs: Women and children, and workers' health. The popular health programs center around vaccination and clean up campaigns. Since December 1981, there have been no cases of polio reported. In 1979, there were 3,784 reported cases of measles, this year so far, only 54 cases.

"The people have volunteered to help with vaccination clinics. For the first time in the history of the world, a whole country was treated for malaria at one time. In order to do this, the whole country had to take a series of three pills at once. In this campaign, 80,000 people volunteered to help distribute pills and explain the process. The medicines were donated by international agencies like WHO (the World Health Organization).

"Since the Revolution new hospitals have been built. The Somoza government shot health care workers and bombed hospitals during the Revolution. Even so, now there are 4 times as many health care centers as under Somoza. But the Contras are destroying health posts deliberately. The value of the health care centers destroyed just in this year, is equal to the entire budget of the health care department."

As she speaks, she grows visibly angry.

"Health care workers are being deliberately killed, kidnapped and terrorized. This is because the health care system has benefited the people and made them happy with the government. The Contras destroy the electricity to places where blood and vaccines are stored. A German and a French doctor were killed recently.

"The other problems in the health care system are that most of the people working in this system are from the old days and they are surly about giving treatment. They miss the corruption from which they benefited. New health workers are being trained but it takes time. This is why the Cuban doctors are needed, but there are doctors from many other countries as well, especially from Europe. Cubans are less than half the number of health workers. In the meantime, [until more are trained?] we are using teaching tools like street theatre and puppet shows for public health education. In 1981, after the floods, the U.S. refused our request for help in setting up a hospital, so the Russians sent a tent hospital. Other than that, there are few Russians in Nicaragua.

"To retrain disabled people is a high priority. Many had polio and, of course, there is disability from the war. There is an organization for the disabled and they have a shop to make wheel chairs. They have made agreements with the taxi drivers to transport disabled people free. There is a school for the blind and a program for early identification of disabled children. There was nothing like this in the past so these things are very exciting.

"In 1979 there were 12,000 shock treatment administered. That was health care under Somoza. Now there are day hospitals where people go for treatment, then they can be with their families at night.

"People here are being taught to recognize alcoholism as a disease. They never did before. Alcoholism was considered normal. We had a terrible accident here on the part of a drunken member of the armed forces. The soldier was punished by giving him 30 years in jail after he killed several people who were in a religious procession. That will make other young people think about drinking and driving.

"Under Somoza, liquor was a great part of the corruption. The generals collected the liquor tax. When I lived on the Rio Coco [a remote region] you couldn't get other things but you could always get rum. Also, now people have a feeling of purpose so that helps people not need to drink.

"My favorite work is the promotion of breast feeding. We do not allow advertising campaigns for formula but some people still use it. Some people think formula is the modern way, but often they put Coca Cola or other things in the bottles. We now have mother's milk banks and women are given time off from work to breast feed."

Cuidad Sandino

As we drive past the famous luxury hotel, the Intercontinental, Mike tells us that it is a good example of how the government got involved in the ownership of some business. Somoza had been a major stockholder in many businesses including the Intercontinental (60%)

so now the government owns his shares. The same management arrangement as before the Revolution continues however, with Pan Am holding the other 40%. Rates are $60 to $100 per night.

The community of Cuidad Sandino is outside of Managua in a flat, dusty area that was once a cotton field. During the time of Somoza, it was a refugee camp for people made homeless by floods and earthquake. There were, at that time, no services, no electricity, no sanitation. Now, as we jounce down the streets, we see power poles leading to each of the neat little houses. We passed the substation on the way into the community. Because services to the poor are a favorite Contra target, there is a guard tower at one end of the substation.

Our bus stops on a dusty side street. We have arrived at our destination, the Maryknoll House. It is a small, tin roofed, wooden house like all the others around it. In the tree shaded back yard we meet with the three nuns who live here. Also present are a young husband and wife, a lay worker team from the U.S. He is a medical doctor; she is a public health worker. Their two small children play in the dirt beneath our chairs.

The wife, pretty despite her no-nonsense short haircut and the fact that she wears exhaustion as casually as other women wear make up, tells us that they don't need to care for the Nicaraguans' health as the government health service provides for that. Their job is to train Salvadoran refugees in health care methods for when they return to El Salvador.

One of the Maryknoll sisters tells us," Before the Revolution people out here suffered terribly because as they united to try to get services, the National Guard would meet them with tear gas. They had no bus service to get to work and no cemetery. When they tried to bury two babies and start a cemetery, the National Guard dug the babies up.

"Now the basic foods are guaranteed them. That's what the ration card is for. It is not really to ration because they could go to the market and buy as much as they want, but to be sure that no one will go hungry. Now people can eat the eggs their chickens lay instead of selling them to buy beans and rice. Children are no longer dying of malnutrition. We used to see baby funerals every day. Now they are rare though still more frequent than in the developed world. But there hasn't been a case of polio in two years and measles is way down."

As we talk, little black chickens stop their scratching in the dirt under the trees and cock their heads to one side, watching us curiously. A small gray cat washes her face.

Another sister continues, "Things are so much better here since the Revolution. We now have garbage pick-up. We never had a garbage truck here before. Some people complain about standing in line for things but they have forgotten awfully quickly how bad it was before. Now they can be outside in the evening, sitting on their porches or walking down the street, where they used to go inside and lock their doors at dark because the National Guard would come around looking for the young people. The reason for price controls and ration cards is to keep people from buying things in large quantities and selling them on the black market."

The young health worker tells how the Sandinistas have tried to deal creatively with shortages. "When Reagan cut off the wheat, we had a big corn promotion. There were corn festivals and bake-offs. The grand prize for the winner of the bake-off was a trip to Corn Island. When there was a rice shortage we had a song on the radio, 'When there is no rice, have some potatoes.' [She sings the cheerful tune.] The attitude is to try new things. Soya is 'the new food for the new man.'"

One of the sisters says, "The people who complain are the ones who don't cooperate with their neighbors."

The health worker's baby crawls into her lap and she cuddles her as she speaks.

"The Contra seem to be trying to ruin everything the government has done. They destroy things you would think that no one with a head and a heart would do, clinics and day care centers.

"My friend's brother, his wife and their seven children were killed because he worked as a C.D.S. [block committees] co-coordinator. Health workers and teachers are also targets. No one attacks military targets. The Contra aren't fighting the military. They run away from direct confrontation with the Sandinista soldiers. Their targets are the civilian population."

[As she speaks, her voice becomes hoarse with emotion.]

"They say that if Congress cuts off funds for the Contras, Reagan will just give the money to Israel and they will give it to the Contras. Two weeks ago when Reagan gave his talk, he told about Freedom Fighters... [her voice breaks entirely and she begins to sob]...the Contras chased a woman and her three children into a ravine and threw a grenade on them...excuse me, I can't help but get emotional. I saw a picture of her with her legs blown off and the bodies of her children huddled against her." [She hugs her own baby tightly and her tears baptize the child's soft hair.]

One of the nuns continues, "I can't even talk to my own sister about this because she wants to believe that the U.S. is the best country and that it can help all other countries. She can't believe that it isn't that way anymore. People in the U.S. deal with these atrocities by saying, 'I don't believe it.'"

The lay worker wipes her eyes with the back of her hand and continues, "I know. I used to have to walk the baby when she had colic. When this happened at work, Salvadoran women would walk with me and tell me their stories. I used to wish the baby would cry harder because I didn't want to hear."

After the meeting, I talk with the lay worker about the letter I've brought from the Salvadoran refugee who lives at our church back in California. She had asked me to look up her sister whom she believes to be in Managua. Yes, she does know the sister, and yes, she will be overjoyed to deliver the letter.

"Only last night she was telling me about her sister in the U.S.," she exclaimed.

We discuss the paper and marking pens I have brought hoping that Nicaraguan children will create messages for our Sunday school classes who have sent messages of peace to them.

"You could take these materials up to the border with you and the children could tell of their experiences with the Contra," she suggests eagerly.

I instantly see that she is right. Of course! Now I have a reason to go to the border. If I can accomplish something, then it is worth the risk.

As we step out of the little house into a street filled with women and children strolling in freedom and security in the soft tropic evening, I hear in my mind the Bible verse I have been waiting for–the verse I can carry with me to the border:

"If we live, we live to the Lord; if we die, we die to the Lord. So whether we live or whether we die, we are the Lord's." (Romans 14:8)

Chapter Nine

A Methodist Missionary and a Human Rights Worker

Wednesday night

One of my objectives in coming to Nicaragua was to meet with our Methodist missionary, Howard Heiner. Howard has some close friends among the members of our church and they asked me to look him up. I am anxious to talk to him myself because a newsletter of his in which he described the brutal murder (by the Contra) of a young health worker, was one of the important factors in my decision to come here.

Finding his house is no problem. We've used it twice now for meetings. Finding him IN the house – that's something else again. Mike must have told him that I want to see him, however, because Howard called this morning and asked if I could meet with him over dinner tonight.

On the way back from Ciudad Sandino the bus leaves me at Howard's house. I wave good-bye to the rest of the group and then stand alone at the curb in the first droplets of a rainstorm; watching the bus grow smaller down the street until it becomes a toy that I could hold in my hand. For the first time since Mexico City, I am really alone.

But not for long. Howard meets me at the door and we drive to a plain but very comfortable restaurant, which, he tells me, is a cooperative. Over hamburgers and coffee, I begin to learn something about this tall, thin man whose name I have heard mentioned with so much respect and affection.

Howard, I discover to my surprise, was born in Sandpoint, Idaho, just twenty miles from the town where my father lives. He is a graduate of the University of Idaho in forestry and knows the woods near my dad's house well, having worked for the Forest Service north of Priest Lake.

Two years ago, Howard and his wife Peggy, a nurse, came to Managua from their previous missionary post in Chile, expecting that Howard would teach forestry at the University. The war has delayed the opening of the Forestry Department, however, and so his work now is with a government forestry project. He has been hoping to organize a tour of Nicaragua for U.S. foresters. There has been considerable interest from these groups in the disruption of Nicaraguan reforestation projects and the deliberate burning of forests by the Contras. U.S. foresters do not like seeing their tax money used to destroy natural resources.

As we discuss the situation here in Nicaragua, Howard tells me that Americans living here have formed a group that meets every Monday to discuss methods of changing U.S. policy toward the Sandinistas. He says it will be a long haul and we must be prepared to think in terms of years.

"North Americans aren't good at patience," he says finishing the last of his small, square hamburger, "We need to learn from the Sandinistas. They began working in 1962 and kept at it all those years."

The waitress refills our cups without a smile. That makes her score perfect–not one smile since we walked in the door. If this is a reflection of how it is to be a waitress in a cooperative, she could give socialism a bad name!

"I understand you're going to Ocotal this weekend," he says.

"That's right," I reply and, trying to sound casual, add, "What's it like there?"

"Well, the best advice for a trip to Ocotal is 'keep your head down.' Last time we were there our Bible study class was punctuated by tracer bullets flying overhead. At the very least you can expect to be hearing lots of machine gun fire."

"Oh," is all I say..

Human Rights Commission - Sister Mary Hartmann

Returning to Howard's house in what has become a drenching downpour, we find the group assembled on the screened porch, listening to Sr. Mary Hartmann's opening remarks:

"I've been in Nicaragua since 1962. I guess you could say I've been converted here. The experience of living with the poor makes you understand what the U.S. is doing in the world and makes you want to do something to prevent injustice."

As this thin, intense woman speaks, rain clatters on the iron porch roof, lighting flashes, and wind jerks the trees back and forth while the blinds slap frantically inside the screens.

"During the time of Somoza, I wondered how it could be that one family could remain in power for 40 years and be so terribly cruel to its people. We had about 90 young people in our parish youth club; about half of them disappeared. Many were found later horribly tortured and mutilated - without eyes or fingernails.

"The Revolution started in June 1979. It didn't get much international press coverage until about 3 weeks later when a U.S. reporter was machine-gunned by a National Guardsman in my neighborhood. That was one North American life, but 50,000 Nicaraguans were also killed in that Revolution. When Somoza left the country, after bombing his own cities, he took the entire treasury with him."

As the clatter of the rain intensifies, I find myself almost glad for its deafening sound. I probably won't want to hear what is coming. And yet I do, as Sister Mary continues:

"One woman I know said to me, 'I lost both of my sons in the Revolution, but it was worth it.' This is what the Nicaraguan people gave - their treasure. You see, people are what they value above all, that is why U.S. visitors always say, 'the people are so friendly.' People are their treasures.

"I heard Reagan say last night on Voice of America that there is a civil war in Nicaragua. There was no war here [since the Revolution] until the U.S. began to fund the Contras in 1980. There is no civil war here. We are being attacked. The U.S. has declared war on Nicaragua. In Reagan's speech, he said there was an anti-government demonstration on Good Friday of 100,000. I was in the Plaza on that day; there were no more than 5,000 and it wasn't an anti-government demonstration. It was a religious procession. Even the U.S. Embassy said it was not an anti-government demonstration and they were reprimanded by the State Department for telling the truth.

"The people who surround Reagan know that Nicaragua is not Communist, that it is not shipping arms to El Salvador, that it is not a threat to the U.S. What is a threat is that if Nicaragua is able to be success-ful, it will be a hope to the poor of all Latin America. If the poor have hope, the multi-national corporations will not be able to exploit them. Nicaragua wants peace. Government officials have offered to go to the U.S. to talk but have been refused visas. Nicaragua has offered to let anyone come and observe and stay as long as they want."

Sister Mary goes on to recount the damage inflicted by the Contra as the rain continues to thunder on the roof.

"One of the many terrible massacres took place in the zone of Waslala. The Contras invaded the home of an agrarian reform leader. They thought they killed the wife - they shot her but she lived to tell the tragedy that happened to her family. They beheaded the six-month-old baby, chopped him up in pieces while he was still alive. Before they burned the crops, they went to the church, burned candles to the Virgin and gave thanks for their victory. This is what has been ordered by the President who ends his speeches by saying 'God bless you.'

A wave of helpless anger floods over me. How does she manage to tell all this without becoming silenced by emotion? She blinks a couple of times and continues:

"They intend to destroy Nicaragua. The mining of the port has not stopped. The cost has been in the millions of dollars of material destruction. There are 1,873 civilians dead: Men, women, and children. Just a few weeks ago, they decapitated an 86-year-old woman. What harm could she have done? It's terrorism against the people of Nicaragua."

Kay, unable to restrain herself any longer blurts out, "But what kind of people could do such butchery?"

Sr. Mary's face twists with pain. "Somoza had a special group of 12 to 15 year olds. One of his greatest crimes is what he did to those boys. They were taken from the country and told they were going to go to the city to be educated. Instead, he trained them in torture. He had more of his people trained in the U.S. Military School in Panama than any other country. Boys from our own neighborhood came back and told how they were trained in torture.

"I work in the prison and I see some of these former National Guardsmen. They can be rehabilitated when they are treated like human beings and they are treated like human beings on these prison farms. They are allowed a week's vacation at home every six months for good conduct. They are taught a trade. These men have not lost their self-respect. Before, all they knew was how to kill, now they can read and write.

"I don't want to give you the idea that Nicaragua is a paradise. There are abuses, but the difference between our human rights commission here and the human rights commissions in El Salvador and Guatemala, is that here we can denounce the abuses and not risk being assassinated. Action will be taken against human rights violators.

"I can honestly say that the central government [Sandinistas] has never swerved from their high ideals on human rights. When violations occur they occur at low levels. If you get the *Americas Watch* for April, the report on the Nicaraguan prison system, the worst violation is that sometimes people are not released when their terms are up. This happened during a Contra offensive last winter because there was fear of an invasion."

This would be right after our invasion of Grenada, I guess.

"People here expect an invasion. They expect it will be a great massacre. They say that the U.S. can send all the bombs it wants, but some people will survive and they will begin again. They will survive."

As she discusses the opposition of some of the Catholic Bishops to the Sandinistas the roar of the rain begins to diminish. Perhaps the worst of the storm is over. Perhaps the most terrible revelations of her report are completed. I hope so. I don't feel I can take much more. A kind of angry numbness threatens and I no longer know if I am actor or bystander. I feel myself implicated in these crimes and yet I am power-less to stop them. Placing guilt was relatively clear-cut at Nuremberg, but how do you assign guilt in a democracy?

Sr. Mary continues, "Bishop Oblando received money from USAID to continue his anti-government activities. They called it 'church development.' The Institute of Religion and Democracy [an American right wing organization of which I have heard many times] gave him $40,000.

"The Pope was not insulted here, the Pope insulted the people. The government made great efforts - spent two weeks gasoline allotment - bringing people to see him. Percentage-wise we had a greater number of people brought to hear the Pope than any Latin American country, but he spoke in a way that the country people did not understand. He said the words, *'iglesia popular'* and the people responded with shouts as they do in the Popular Mass. When he said *'silencio,'* the people were shocked. They hadn't meant it as disrespect, but it was reported as disrespect. Afterwards 500 base communities wrote to the Pope begging his pardon for whatever they did to offend him, but they never received a reply.

"There were other incidents that hurt people. The mother of Daniel Ortega was pushed out of line by one of the Bishops and not allowed to receive Communion from the Pope. She is a traditional Catholic and had looked forward to the Pope's visit from the time it was announced. She was heartbroken.

"This is a very Christian government. You know after the Revolution there was no bloodbath as followed so many revolutions. That's amazing when you consider the brutality that preceded it. We kept hearing on the radio, in the days after the Revolution, that no one would be allowed to take the law into his own hands. Tomas Borge stopped the lynching of an ex-National Guardsman by saying, 'if we do to them what they did to us, why did we have this revolution?'"

A Bad Night

Just in the short distance from house to bus, we had all gotten thoroughly soaked. The mood on the bus, as it splashed through the dark streets was damp and grim. A few people began to argue about whether or not the stories of atrocities that we heard today should be repeated at home.

"No one will believe us," a voice contends in the dark. "They won't want to hear it and they'll turn off on everything we say."

"But we have an obligation..."

The voices go on and I look out the window into the dark, which seemed far more profound than usual. Cheryl, Hal's fiancée, slips into the seat next to me. She had flown in to join the group only yesterday, health problems having kept her from leaving with everyone else.

"Hal and I are going to get married here in Nicaragua," she says. "Of course it won't be legal, but we'll redo the ceremony when we get home."

"That's terrific," I say, glad to have something to be happy about.

"We decided today that we are going to have the ceremony tomorrow night in Revolutionary Plaza and we'd like you to be our Matron-of-Honor."

"Why thank you! I'd be delighted!"

We continue with a discussion of wedding plans until suddenly the bus comes to an abrupt stop. It is pitch dark all around us. Why are we stopping out here in the country? Then Mike announces that we are actually back at the hotel, but that all the electricity is off in this sector of the city. No one knows why. It could be sabotage. It could be just the storm. Or could it also be, I wonder silently, the beginning of an invasion by the U.S.? How strange it would be to be killed by the very bombs one has helped to purchase!

We dig flashlights out of pockets and purses and find our way to our rooms. To save on batteries (unavailable here) I shower in the pitch dark. I wonder if my friend, the Paul Bunyan size cockroach, has crawled out of the drain and is wandering around ready to jump onto my feet. I am so hot and sticky though, that I no longer care what creatures I share the shower with as long as I get clean in the process!

Although Leticia, who has missed the evening meeting, seems nearly asleep as I come in, she is anxious to hear what had transpired. I play my tape of Sr. Mary's testimony for her. Lying there in the dark, with no reality but the disembodied voice of the nun, the effect of the terrible stories is even more devastating than previously. I know Leticia must be deeply upset, also. We turn off the player as the tape finishes and are lingering on the edge of sleep when the lights, the fan, and

Leticia's tape player all spring to life so abruptly that we both leap several inches into the air. We giggle a little at ourselves as we turn everything off and try to go back to sleep.

At last, the even breathing from Leticia's bed tells me that she is asleep. Ironically, now that I have finally decided that I do not want to get sick after all, I feel that unmistakable chewing sensation in the pit of my stomach that I learned to recognize in Peru. I fumble through my purse to find the pills I've brought for just such an occasion. I swallow some of them, without water, but they are only making me sicker. Shaking and sweating, I can barely manage to navigate the 3 or 4 feet from bed to bathroom. As I write, my body feels so heavy that it seems about to press its way down through the cot pad and into the springs.

Illness merges into nightmares and drains away the rest of the night.

Chapter Ten

From the U.S. Embassy to Corinto

Thursday morning

I awake feeling like an inflatable toy might feel, having been deflated and flattened, to find itself once again three-dimensional. I am better. Weak, but better. Definitely better....

Rain must have fallen most of the night because the hotel owner's wife is using a broom to sweep great pools of water from the courtyard tiles into the planted rectangles. The rectangles no longer show dirt and grass, only iron gray water reflecting a pale, featureless sky.

The barber has come to shave the hotel owner as he does every day. He carries his tools in a medical bag and the operation is carried out in the open end of the lobby nearest the courtyard. The masculine monosyllabic chatter of the two men heard above the whisking sound of the broom provides a relaxing melody of normalcy, a welcome counterpoint to last night's horror.

Today's first item of business will be a visit to the U.S. Embassy to join a vigil by U.S. citizens living in Nicaragua. This is the 6-month "anniversary" of these demonstrations which have been taking place every Thursday, rain or shine, since shortly after the Grenada invasion which Reagan announced as a way to, "evacuate medical students."

At the Embassy

Our bus must park a block away from the embassy because the road has been blocked off by Nicaraguan police who are certainly most anxious to avoid an incident that could provoke U.S. retaliation. We pick our way carefully across a muddy field (the embassy is in a section of town that is mostly empty land) and see that a crowd of several hundred has already gathered in front of the massive iron gates. The demonstrators all appear to be North Americans.

A street theatre troupe cavorts to the cheers of the crowd. One of the actors is dressed as Uncle Sam in an outrageously tall hat. He holds the strings of another actor playing a puppet. The puppet wears a sign around his neck identifying him as "Honduras."

We have missed most of the speeches but as we arrive one speaker, a woman, is concluding. She addresses the crowd in English telling them that they must continue their efforts to stop U.S. support for the Contras. The program concludes with a poetry reading and a moment of silence. The new ambassador arrived last night. Ambassadors are recalled quickly here, the last one having served less than a year. The reason, according to Mike, is that when they start sending home reports containing the truth about Nicaragua, they get fired.

After the crowd begins to break up, I see several people I know. Three of them are missionaries who I met in Peru and another is a recent president of Church Women United in Pasadena. She introduces me to another couple who turn out to be friends of some of our church members and also to another man, an American who lives in Managua. As we talk, he finds out that I am going to Ocotal. He looks at me intensely and says, "Duck. That's the watchword at the border – just DUCK!"

The Port of Corinto

At mid-morning we set off in our bus for the port city of Corinto, where the harbor was recently mined by the CIA. Soon after leaving Managua we pass a training camp for soldiers. It is tiny and almost innocently rustic in comparison with even small military bases in the U.S.

We pass acres and acres of fields growing corn. Rusting cotton-processing equipment bears mute testimony to the change of land use. Under Somoza for every acre that grew food, twenty-two acres grew export crops such as cotton, beef, and sugar. The profits from the sale of these crops went to him, to his friends, and to his corporate sponsors in the United States.

In places the land, so long drained by exhaustive cotton growing, has been replanted in trees; eucalyptus trees for fuel, fruit trees for food. A deep sweet smell flows in the open windows of our little bus. A billboard advises, "Alcoholism causes accidents." Huge new storage barns fly past and the smell of soy enters the bus.

Cooperative farms, recognizable by their neat groupings of new cinderblock buildings, appear tidy and comfortable. Outside of a new school building children study around a large table under a poinciana tree which glows with intensely orange blossoms. Cotton can still be seen growing between fields of food crops, but no longer is it a blight on the land and a prison for the people.

During the 1950's, Somoza saw to it that cotton investors got cheap bank credit because he personally gained millions from the export trade. Cotton took over most of the Pacific plain. The farmers were evicted and forced to labor long hours in choking dust and pesticides under the broiling sun where the temperature ran to over 100 degrees. For this they were paid far less than a living wage. In the midst of fertile farmland, malnutrition was endemic.

As the bus rolls on, the flatness of the cotton growing areas gives way to low hills. We pass older villages of square houses, some with tile roofs, others with roofs of pale thatch. In the tree shaded farmyards cattle, pigs, geese and chickens abound. Small adobe houses appear and disappear in our windows – too quickly for my imagination to take up residence within them as I long to do. I want to try on the garments and the lives of their owners. But we pass too quickly to seize anything but a fleeting smell of onion and a patch of dappled shade.

As we approach Corinto, the bus dips down again onto the coastal plain. It seems remarkable to me that during our travels both today and Sunday, we have never been stopped for identity checks. My experience in South America and the experiences of friends in Honduras and El Salvador was that in most of Latin America such roadblocks and document checks are routine. If Nicaragua is practicing "internal terrorism against its own people," it sure isn't very thorough about it.

We enter the island on which the port city of Corinto sits, over a bridge guarded by armed soldiers. There have been many attempts by the Contra to blow up this bridge. Until the port was mined, 80% of all the imported goods coming into Nicaragua passed over this low, two lane bridge.

Like any port city, Corinto is dirty. The one and two story buildings that crowd together along narrow streets have a down-at-the-heels, skuzzy look. Mike says that the city is much better than it was during the time of Somoza, however. Then the National Guard and the Somoza family controlled the entire drug and prostitute trade as well as the saloons that were a fixture in every block of the city. Now the drug traffic has been greatly reduced and the prostitutes are being retrained for jobs as secretaries and clerks.

We alight from the bus in the center of a crowded, grimy square. All eyes are immediately fixed on us. It is a horrible feeling. This is the city that U.S. planes fly over every day. We have closed their port, removed their livelihood, blown up their fuel storage depot. I don't really expect them to be glad to see us.

One man pushes past us muttering, "*ricas rubias*! [rich blondies]"

Leticia shouts after him, "We're not rich, we're just people like you!"

We keep walking through the marketplace, smiling resolutely, and soon the scowling faces relent. People begin to smile back. We stop at a little fruit stand. Leticia buys three limes and strikes up a conversation with the proprietress.

The lady's face is lined and tired. "I have terrible headaches all the time," she says. "It's because we are always afraid of another attack. The planes fly over every day from Honduras. They are CIA planes. We are afraid all the time that they will drop bombs on us."

Leticia, Sister Mary Catherine, and I walk through the narrow streets stopping occasionally in the dark, bare little shops. One store sells books, many of which are dirty. Oh, I don't mean "X" rated—I mean dirty as in gray and shopworn. This city is suffering economic depression like nothing we've seen in Nicaragua, but people are still reading whatever they can get.

As the three of us round a corner, we see Marilyn in the midst of a crowd of school children on their way home from school. She is reading to them from a pop-up book she has brought along. We begin to take pictures of the gathering and the kids crowd around us with delight. Picking up their schoolroom chairs (which they have to carry back and forth with them each day) they accompany us all the way back to the bus. We give them nothing but our friendship and they do not ask for more. I can't help remembering the crowds of children I have encountered in other Third World countries who mob visitors with begging that quickly, sometimes frighteningly, morphs into demanding.

A young government official hops on the bus with us and rides along to the fuel docks so that we can inspect the damage our tax dollars have purchased. Like all the government personnel we have encountered, he is friendly, open, and polite.

The three storage tanks destroyed in last October's attack, look as if they had been collapsed by a giant fist. Piles of twisted metal and fused concrete stand bleakly above the empty, gray harbor. And yet, as gruesome as the damage is, it is not anywhere near as total as news reports have led us to believe. Seven large drums still remain. Only through the heroic efforts of the defense teams were these kept from exploding. At the time of the attack, they had been filled with high-octane aviation fuel and had they caught fire the whole city of 27,000 people would have been at risk. All of those people trying to escape over the one, thin bridge! I wonder how many of those friendly little kids would have made it?

Or how many will make it next time. The city has been bombed several times. On the anniversary of the Revolution last year (July 19) a 500 pound bomb was dropped. Through amazing luck no damage was done.

"Every day spy planes go over taking pictures," the young man tells us. "In September of 1983 they bombed the port facilities again, then in October they attacked by boat and did this damage. Two months ago they attacked us for 3 days and nights by boat, but we managed to hold them off."

The young man continues to talk as we climb through the rubble. A smiling young soldier pauses from his sentry duty to pose for a picture with Cheryl.

"The U.S. says it has stopped the mining, but mines are still out there. They are dropped by helicopter at night. A CIA ship is anchored just 20 miles out there... [he points to the gray horizon]...and planes and helicopters take off from it."

We scrape the cinders from our feet as we reboard the bus.

The government official accompanies us to lunch in a restaurant on the square. Most of the group are eating generous portions of fish. I'm still not feeling what you'd call robust, so I just order rice. As we eat, the young man answers questions:

"In Somoza's time, Corinto had 200 cantinas and only 2 schools," he says.

"How many international groups like ours come to see the damage here?" I ask, picking at the rice.

"Probably 2 or 3 a week. Mostly European, especially Germans," he says.

While he and Hal carry on a rapid conversation in Spanish, Leticia turns to me and says; "You see how polite and humble he is, well in the old days a government official would never eat with us like this. They walked around all the time with the stars on their chests and their big stomachs sticking out and never gave anybody so much as the right time of day!"

On the road back to Managua, we pass the largest Soviet installation in Nicaragua. It is a tent hospital that the Russians sent after the 1982 flood. Nicaragua had asked us (that is the U.S.) first for medical help, but "we" refused. In any case, the hospital doesn't appear very impressive. It's just a small cluster of tents in a field, like the hospital in "*M.A.S.H.*"

From A Supermarket to A Unique Wedding

We were supposed to visit the American Embassy this afternoon. Our appointment was at four but we were late getting back from Corinto so that when we arrived, a little before 4:30, we found the Embassy closing. They wouldn't let us in.

We were disappointed, but went instead to another shopping center to observe more daily life. I wandered off by myself and decided to do some housewife-ly Fact Finding by investigating a supermarket.

What I expected to find was row upon row of empty shelves, as had been the case in Peru, but to my surprise the shelves were full! There was not a great variety of items, but all the necessities were there - and cheap! Plenty of rice, beans, and chicken was in evidence. I bought coffee (a little less than a pound) for less than a dollar.

The store itself was bright, spacious and decorated by large colorful murals of Indian harvests. There was none of the tight security, complete with armed men on high platforms that I used to find so oppressive when I did the grocery shopping in Peru. In Peru, in 1979, a sign could read, "shoplifters will be shot."

Now we are back at the hotel and everyone is hurrying to change clothes for Hal and Cheryl's wedding. While I was touring the supermarket, they were getting a wedding cake at the bakery.

We pile into the bus again putting Hal in the front and Cheryl in the back in order to preserve some semblance of tradition. At Revolutionary Plaza we all climb out and head, in masse, for the eternal flame that honors the intellectual father of the Revolution, Carlos Fonseca Amador. Such is our faith in the lack of brutality of the army that no one worries about the attitude of the three gun-toting soldiers guarding the monument. It is hard to believe that I was so apprehensive about getting off the bus here while the militia drilled less than a week ago!

As the vows are exchanged, I look at our little congregation standing in a semi-circle in front of us. It is strange indeed to see the three armed soldiers standing respectfully among the wedding guests! After the service, they join the informal receiving line and shake hands with the couple as they add their congratulations to those of the rest of us. They even allow themselves to be photographed with the newly weds. Marilyn has brought her concertina and she plays an Irish jig. The soldiers join in the laughter as the new bride dances.

We return to the hotel for a bridal dinner of chicken and pasta, cucumber salad, rice, bread, and wedding cake. There are a few small gifts and much laughter and joy.

Chapter Eleven

We Meet With a Commandante and Salvadoran Refugees

Friday Morning

Although the party was still going strong at ten o'clock last night, I wasn't. I still wasn't feeling very well, so I excused myself and went to bed. It seemed I had been sleeping for hours when I heard a loud knock at the door.

"Come in," I croaked.

It was Marilyn. "Sorry to wake you," she said, "but I just had to tell everyone – we just heard, the Senate voted to cut off aid for the Contras!"

I thanked her, thanked God, and slept very soundly.

Today is a lovely day! The rectangles of reflected sky in the courtyards are blue again. A light breeze rattles the banana leaves. A radio somewhere is playing the Exodus theme, my memory supplies the words, "this land is mine." Maybe that will be true now for the Nicaraguans. Leticia says I told her all about the Senate decision last night when she came in (I don't remember doing that!) but she didn't know whether to believe me because she knew I was asleep. She hadn't heard the news because she'd been visiting relatives since shortly after dinner.

Bob, Mike and Evan are eating breakfast in the lobby and they confirm that I had not been dreaming. Marilyn told them also. Maybe this is a new beginning for Nicaragua!

Commandante Raphael Soliz, President; Foreign Relations Committee

Outside the Council of State Building, I use my last pictures in case they decide to open our cameras this time. No one does, though, and as we walk up the wide stairs to the second floor conference room, Mike gives us some quick background on the Council of State:

"Until the November elections, the Council of State will remain the legislative governing body of the country. There are 57 seats representing all the recognized political parties and interest groups such as labor, women, students, and private business. The churches had representation too, but withdrew because of their belief in the separation of church and state."

We rise as the Commandante enters the conference room, but he smiles and motions for us to sit. He is a youngish man, probably in his thirties; dark, mustached, and clad in the famous Sandinista uniform. As he sits next to me, I can see deep lines of fatigue etched into his youthful face. After the opening pleasantries, he says:

"In the new government, after the November elections, we will have a total of 90 representatives; 27 from Managua, 8 from the Atlantic Coast (four of them Miskitu Indians.) Up to now five parties have announced their official participation in the elections. The remaining four recognized parties have not decided if they will participate or abstain. Of course, the elections are being carried out under difficult circumstances because we are in a state of war particularly in the north where there is combat being carried out."

Oh yes, The North. Where we are going tomorrow! We are all being served coffee in little glass cups. The Commandante is served only in turn and service has begun at the opposite end of the table from him. Interestingly enough there are no bodyguards or whatever the equivalent of the Secret Service is here.

"We hope the American people will take a position that will prevent Reagan's aggression during our election."

He speaks in a soft baritone.

"We hope many people from the U.S. will come here and talk to people from all sectors of our society and all levels of the church. The Catholic hierarchy is opposed to the Revolution but many priests support it. We hope that relations will improve with the U.S. We see as a very positive sign the vote in the House of Representatives yesterday against funding for the Contras."

So it wasn't the Senate after all. What a terrible disappointment! We had all known ahead of time that the House would not approve it. With a stalemate like this, the administration will find a way to continue to support the Contra.

"We think that better relations with the U.S. are very important, that is why we are willing to speak to any delegation that wishes to come."

Question: "Will there be a serious disruption of the election if the parties on the right withdraw?"

He looks sad, "Yes, it would be a disruption but it would not stop the elections.

Question: "Will voting be compulsory as it is in El Salvador?"

"No, only registration will be compulsory. Voting will be voluntary."

"How will the election campaigns be financed?"

"Six million cordobas will be given to each party. They can also raise their own money. Some parties like the Social Christians are affiliated with international organizations. There will be no limit on the amount of money any party can spend."

[He takes off his glasses and rubs his eyes frequently. He seems very tired.]

Bill asks, "yesterday, in Corinto, we saw a poster for the Marxist-Leninist Party saying that the Sandinistas were not giving them political freedom. Is this true?"

He smiles faintly, "There are two parties we call 'extreme left;' this is one of those. We have not given this party representation because its position is that all parties should not be able to participate in government, but only the leftist parties. Also, they believe that only workers and peasants should be allowed to have representation. We consider this too extreme so we do not recognize this party."

Question: "What concessions are you willing to make to end the conflict with the US '?"

"We are willing to freeze the level of arms in our country at present levels, but we believe that this should be done in all of Central America. El Salvador and Honduras say this would be to their disadvantage, however they have a constant influx of U.S. arms which they do not pay for."

Through the "training exercises" as well as outright grants?

Question: "Is Nicaragua supplying arms to the rebels in El Salvador?"

"We do not supply arms to them to fight their government, but we do not arrest Salvadorans who come into our territory. Our country has no bases of the Salvadoran rebels, but Honduras and Costa Rica both have bases in their country from which the Contra attack us.

Question: "President Reagan says there are 10,000 Cubans in Nicaragua. Would you comment on that?"

Commandante Soliz smiles. "That is pure rhetoric. He has never been able to give any evidence of that. We have had an average of about 200 advisors here. That is nothing like the 3,000 U.S. advisors in Honduras."

Question: "Do you have a Marxist government in Nicaragua?"

"The Marxist accusation has no basis in fact. We believe that Marxism is a useful tool of social analysis. We are not even considering forming a single party system in Nicaragua. We believe that there is no contradiction between having many parties represented and building a better society for all the people. After the election, we will continue to have a mixed economy. Even though there is now government planning of the economy, we have 60% private sector. The Communists accuse us of having a Capitalist economy because we find no need to have a controlled state economy like Russia or Eastern Europe."

Back at the hotel, I collapse on the bed to rest before lunch. I am weak and shaky – given to fits of sweating. I hope I last out the weekend. Ironic! I got my wish to be sick, but now I am determined to go to the war zone anyhow!

Friday afternoon

We stop at the Museum of the Literacy Campaign to examine the materials. These books certainly are not teaching Communism. They are, however, highly nation-alistic. Along with many, many pages of materials which simply use the everyday experiences of poor farmers to teach basic skills like math and phonics (along the lines of Paolo Friere) are some stories that seem to point to the need to keep Nicaraguan land and resources for the benefit of Nicaraguans. I suppose that could be pretty upsetting to some people!

Mike tells us of a time when he was with a group at the U.S. Embassy and the literacy materials were being shown to them. A page on which was a picture of a man with a rifle was flashed past them as evidence that the literacy campaign was fostering militarism. Mike said, "Wait, let's read that!" And, after turning back to the page in question, they read the text. What it said was, "Carlos is going to the hills to shoot birds, but we don't need to kill birds because we don't have to eat them."

The most shattering thing in the museum, though, is the Hall of Heroes and Martyrs. It is a large room with framed photos of young people hanging on all four walls. There are perhaps 50, all caught in typical youthful poses: some smiling, some dreamy. The birth dates on the plaques under the pictures range from 1958 to 1966. The common denominator is that they were all killed while teaching literacy or basic health care. Some of them died in accidents but many were killed by the Contras. In glass cases under the photos are "relics" – here a worn pair of tennis shoes, there a neatly folded tee shirt. In one case sits a yellow cap with the letters CAT on the front. Some of these tennis shoes are so heartbreakingly small!

On the way to our next stop, we spend a few minutes at a union hall while our bus driver goes off to try to find gasoline. Men and women, mostly young, are gathering for a meeting. They look at us curiously and smile. We browse through the little union bookstore. Side by side are Marx and the complete works of Shakespeare in Spanish.

We are off again and ride for some time before we reach one of the many neighborhoods of low-lying houses that ring the devastated heart of the city. At a church, we find a workshop where perhaps a dozen Salvadoran refugees are hard at work making belts and purses out of leather. We stop to pick up the American missionary who will be our guide out to the farm where many Salvadoran refugees are living. We also stop because this is where the sister of the Salvadoran refugee who lives at our church is working.

As I enter the unenclosed porch filled with leather scraps and voices, I immediately know the woman I am looking for. The family resemblance is so strong that I see without asking that she is my friend's sister. Perhaps because of this instant recognition, we embrace as if we had met before.

After some exchange of information and picture taking, she gives me a purse and some books for her sister and I return to the bus after one final hug, "This is for my sister," she says.

When I return to the bus the first thing I do is to apologize for making everyone wait in the heat. They are all touched by the story of the separated sisters, though, and said they didn't mind.

Refugee Resettlement

The co-operative farm, now owned by the Salvadoran refugees, was once part of a Somoza estate. The Sandinistas have given title to this group of about 150 people. It is rolling, lovely land, dotted with huge trees. Chickens wander freely, pecking at the dirt while children play on modern playground equipment in the shade of one of the trees. Pigs root in their thatch shaded pen as the lowing of cattle mingles with the laughter of children and the crowing of roosters. The bloody conflict from which these people have comes seems like a grotesque dream.

But it is no dream. Two men, thin and tense as antelope, meet us as we stride from the bus toward the farm buildings. "No photographs!" They tell us. Their faces are full of the nightmares they have seen. In spite of their obvious respect for our guide, they do not want us to tour their farm.

And so we stand in the dusty lane while our guide tells us about the resettlement project.

"The people here have been growing tomatoes and onions. The state buys everything that the co-op members don't use for themselves, that way they don't have to worry about marketing. A project has recently been started to sell eggs. Those new chicken farm buildings were constructed with development funds from Norway. And over here... [he gestures towards a giant fig tree] they have an open-air school for the children. A pre-school has been started, too."

On the way out of the farm, we take a narrow loop road through the area where the families live in their modest, but new, homes. Each house has a front door in the middle and a window on each side of the door. Most have neatly fenced flower gardens in front. This certainly is a contrast with the pictures I have seen of the crowded and sordid conditions of the refugee camps in Honduras. Another contrast - these refugees are free to go wherever they please within Nicaragua, rather than being virtual prisoners as are the refugees in the Honduran camps.

Friday evening

Two new dishes for dinner tonight! One is a cooked squash, like zucchini only denser; cut in rounds, cooked, and topped with grated egg. The other is a cold, sweetened beet juice. It may not sound good; but it was.

Tonight as I pack for our trip to the war zone, a cockroach the length of a man's longest finger peaked over the edge of my bed where I have my clothes laid out. He twitches his feelers a couple of times and then scurries up the sheet and over my pillow. I know I have to get rid of him, but if I squash him, he'll make such a mess I'll have to sleep on the floor. I grabb a book from my nightstand and herd him off the bed and onto the floor. My idea is to usher him out the door and into the courtyard with minimum damage to the sensibilities of both him and me.

He is having none of my queasy humanitarianism, however, and when he realizs that he is being shown to the door he bolts around the edge of my book and races back in the direction of my bed. Seeing no choice, I grit my teeth and stomp on him. The mess is horrible!

As I write, smaller bugs occasionally hop on the foot of my bed. I just pull myself up into a ball and ignore them. If I killed them, it would only be to make room for their replacements. There are always more bugs. I'm just thankful that I am usually too tired to feel whatever crawls on me while I am asleep.

And sleep I must because tomorrow is the day of the long trip to the north. Before I turn out the light, I hold Dave's picture in my hand for many minutes. I was going to leave it here in Managua with my extra clothes because the frame is ceramic and fragile, but instead I slip it into my purse. Funny how comforting that one small act is.

Chapter Twelve

Into The War Zone

Saturday morning

Neither Leticia nor I slept well last night. She got up at four a.m. to pack to visit her sister in Matagalpa. She's not going with us to Ocotal because she's worried about her sister who is a diabetic and must have protein. The Matagalpa area has been under attack by Contra and so meat deliveries have been delayed. Leticia is going to take canned meat and fish to her sister.

I had trouble sleeping partly because of apprehension about the trip but mostly because, although I feel much better, some creatures, it seems, are holding a dance marathon inside my stomach. At least that's how it feels!

No one else is up yet. It's a few minutes after six, and so I am sitting in the courtyard enjoying the early morning relative coolness. Birds are chirping and the banana leaves rattle softly. An early rising fly inscribes lazy circles in the air.

Last night, as I lay staring into the dark and listening to the metallic complaints from our fan, my mind kept returning to the dead teenagers whose photographs hang in the Museum of the Literacy Campaign and to the slaughtered children of teachers and community leaders in the north. The temptation for North Americans is to put such stories down to over-enthusiasm by ill-trained Contra troops. But the truth is that such terrorism is neither random nor acciden-tal. It is a deliberate strategy to intimidate anyone who attempts to carry out the programs of the Nicaraguan government. It is, after all, one thing for a dedicated public official to elect to risk his own life, but to risk the lives of his whole family is quite another. To cut up the 6-month-old baby of one community leader is to send a message to all other community leaders in the area.

What we in the U.S. must recognize is that this strat-egy has the blessing of our State Department. Men and women whose salaries we pay planned, and are carrying out, this slaughter of the innocents.

Part of the problem, too, is that when we hear of atrocities in Latin America our subconscious racism is activated. Dave and I heard former Ambassador to El Salvador, Deane Hinton; speak in Aspen two years ago. He explained to the audience "these people, descen-dants of Mayans who believed in human sacrifice, are inherently violent."

But the violence is not in the people; the violence is in the system. How else can people who are already dying of starvation because they don't have enough land to feed themselves, be frightened into submis-sion? Threats of death are not enough because perhaps a quick death would be preferable to them to a slow death by malnutrition and disease. No, there must also be unbearable pain and degradation. That is the rea-son for atrocities and torture.

If we intend to place our political and military power behind preserving the status quo in Latin America, we had better understand that we are also locking ourselves into irrevocable partnership with torturers.

Hal and Cheryl are sitting down to breakfast and they ask me to join them. As we drink the strong native coffee Hal says, "You know when Cheryl and I went out by ourselves last night we went to this restaurant, and well there were some Nicaraguan men at the table next to us having a really interesting conversation..."

"So we listened," Cheryl says, with a grin.

"Couldn't help overhearing, you know. They were talking about the U.S., kind of discussing the pros and cons of our system. One of them seemed to be supporting it and another one was saying, 'You've been to Washington and New York, you know how miserably the poor live there...'"

"Another man," Cheryl added, "said that the U.S. is like Rome and Reagan is Caesar. This guy got really upset and started waving his arms around and talking about imperialism."

We finish breakfast and I start back to my room to collect my things. Cheryl and Herb are not going to Ocotal, the long trip being too much for Cheryl' bad back. As I leave the narrow breezeway-dining room, I pass quite close to the table where three women with crisply British accents are eating breakfast. They have been staying here several days, but they haven't gone out of their way to be friendly. I get the feeling they aren't crazy about North Americans. In pursuit of Facts, I initiate a conversation with them anyhow.

"Oh, yes," the dark haired one says, we come here often from our headquarters in Mexico City. We're from Oxfam."

I see my impression was correct. They are very critical of U.S. policy regarding Nicaragua. They don't blame me personally, however, and we have a nice conversation. An Oxfam ship will be docking soon on the Atlantic Coast with tools and agricultural supplies.

Toward Ocotal with a Stop at the Mechanical School

The bus arrives at a little after eight and we begin to load luggage on the top. We're not taking much ourselves, but there are several suitcases full of supplies for the missionaries living there. Someone remarks that they feel quite safe on this journey because "no one would shoot North Americans." I wonder how a land mine would know what passports the bus passengers are carrying, but I keep the thought to myself.

Twenty or thirty miles north of Managua, we move into the highlands. The road is two lane, blacktopped and smoother than most, perhaps because it is the main road north and is important in moving supplies. I feel right at home as the scenery looks just like Southern California: dry with low, shrubby underbrush.

The bus sounds like it is really struggling already on the hills. I wish I didn't know that the brakes are bad. I had to take an anti-histamine pill this morning because my left eye is all swollen. That probably wasn't such a good idea though, as it adds to my dehydration from illness. Further, on we stop at a gas station where several preadolescent businessmen board the bus selling fruit juice in plastic bags.

Now we are leaving the blacktop, jolting along a dirt road. We're looking for the agricultural mechanical school that we are supposed to visit, but Mike and his wife are not sure where it is. There is some tension apparently, and this tension increases as we stop in a village and a truckload of armed soldiers watch us. One has his rifle trained in our direction.

All is well, though. After traveling over some suspiciously rickety bridges, we see a sign pointing toward the school. Another turn in the road and here we are! It is quite an idyllic spot. A large hacienda surrounded by verandas upstairs and down, is the main building. Students are practicing driving John Deere tractors in the shade of an enormous tree. Just outside the compound, in a dusty field, a herd of cattle is being driven by a cowboy on a burro.

On the cool veranda, we are greeted by the young, blue-eyed American from Florida who is in charge of the school. His name is Fred. Behind him, taped to the wall, a hand made sign with a picture of Sandino and the words, "fifty years," flutters in the breeze.

"This ranch," he tells us, in his soft, Cracker accent, "belonged to a high level Somoza general who sold the property when he saw that the Revolution was about to succeed. After the Triumph, he was jailed because he had been renting plots of land to peasants, allowing them to plant and develop the land, and then evicting them and selling the crops himself. [I've read about this practice, evidently a favorite trick of the landowners. After he was released from jail, he went to Miami.

How strange! The Nicaraguan goes to Florida and the Floridian takes his place on the Nicaraguan ranch!

"A new government project to develop land that is stumpy or rocky has begun. The headquarters will be in Dano, which is Eden Pastora's hometown and quite conservative. That headquarters will employ a lot of people and many of them are training here right now."

Bob asks, "Do you have a problem getting spare parts for these tractors?"

"You know, it's funny," Fred answers with a grin, "but commerce goes on no matter what. Right now International Harvester is happy to sell to anyone, so spare parts are no problem!"

"Are you feeling any effects of Contra attacks here?"

"In November there was an ambush by Contra just seven km from here. Two co-op members were killed and so were all twelve Contras. We are having problems getting cement because so many people have had to be moved from border areas and new housing has to be built for them. It's the old Socialist problem; things are not expensive - it's just that you can't find them. I think that's better though than having them plentiful and expensive because this way they can be assigned to where they are needed most. We'll have the cement we need soon. It's really not a serious problem."

We move off the veranda and into the shade of the trees. Although I know we are very close to the Equator, it still seems strange to me to see the sun directly overhead! The students mingle with us. One of them is a pretty young girl wearing a khaki uniform. A black and red Sandinista scarf is tied around her neck. We seat ourselves on rocks and bricks as several students thank us for coming.

Mike translates, "It means a lot to have people from the U.S. come to visit us in friendship and we hope more will come."

At the end of the second floor veranda, I can see a chalkboard. The word, "objectives," in Spanish, is inscribed at the top and a list is neatly written under it.

A student named Roberto says, "We worked for many years in factories in Managua. We knew how things worked, but not why. Now we are learning theory for the first time. We want to learn how to do things correctly."

"How do you support your families while you attend school?"

Another student, an older man named Ignacio, says, "Our government pays us a salary to go to school. In spite of the aggression and suffering in this country, we are trying to pull ourselves up by our fingernails. You see, our government believes that it does no good to defend ourselves at the border and let the economy fall apart, so they pay us the same wage we were earning at the jobs we left."

Carlos, tall and thin with a deeply lined face says, "In Nicaragua until now there has been anarchy in terms of salaries. Now, with the new arrangement, those areas hardest hit by inflation get raises. The goal is to adjust salaries to the level of productivity of the business and the individual. In the past the owner's brother-in-law would get a big salary for doing nothing and the workers would get paid too little to live on. Now the goal is to adjust pay so that people in the country can earn the same as those in the cities."

A boy named Rigoberto says, "Real salaries are measured not only in terms of money but also benefits like health care and low cost stores."

Says Juan, "The ideal is to make things better for those who have never had enough. It wouldn't help to have them earn more if productivity doesn't rise also. The government would just have to raise the prices of basic foods. It's for that reason that unions have commissaries where people can buy at reduced prices. This also prevents speculators from buying large quantities and pushing prices up."

"Do unions have the right to strike?"

"In a Revolutionary society there is no reason for a strike," Juan answers. "In the old days we had to go on strike for higher wages, but now the government is working in our behalf. A strike against the private sector would not be good either, because it would be bad for the economy. Instead we discuss the problem and try to work it out."

From inside the hacienda comes the "click, click, click, thunk" of a ping-pong game. An elderly man named Annibal tells how this large building was only a weekend home for the Somocista owner, and how it was guarded by soldiers and dogs.

We troop across the farmyard and out to the new workshop built of cement blocks and corrugated iron.

Inside everything is neat, clean, and organized. Large new machines stand here and there on the cement floor.

"We get this equipment from hunger projects around the world," Fred tells us.

Inside, the hacienda is one big, open room except for a partitioned off area at one end where new wooden bunks can be glimpsed. The dining hall portion is furnished with picnic tables where we sit and share the students' lunch with them. There certainly seems to be plenty. Huge portions of rice, beans, and a delicious cabbage dish with onion and chicken are served along with large corn tortillas. As we finish our lunches, a girl student wallops a young man at ping-pong.

The far end of the room is set up as a classroom with wide-armed schoolroom chairs and a blackboard. I ask Fred what organization brought him to Nicaragua. "None," he says, "my wife and I just wanted to come here so we did it on our own savings."

Back on the road again, Evan tells us that the girl who had been playing ping-pong had recently been out on patrol when they captured five Contras. Three of the Contra, she said, were American citizens. The patrol turned them over to their superior officers and she believes the men were sent home.

As we retrace our route through the tiny village, I see that the soldiers are gone. Looking down the one dusty main street, I notice a sign over the front door of one of the adobe buildings. It says "health center."

The main road is smooth and, as we climb higher into the mountains toward Esteli, I begin to doze. Suddenly I sit up straight.

"Big Pine!" I say out loud.

"What?" says Kay who is sitting next to me.

"Big Pine!" I repeat, "the code name for the U.S. military maneuvers in Honduras."

Kay is still looking puzzled.

"Remember how Fred was telling us that before the U.S. companies logged it over, there were big pine forests in the area the Contras are trying to take – the place where we are going – and that the name of the main town, the one they are trying to capture for a provisional capital, has a name that means 'Fat Pine.' He told us *ocotal* means 'Fat Pine' in Spanish. Well, maybe it is a coincidence that the U.S. military exercises are called 'Big Pine', but it sure is interesting!"

Our bus moves slowly uphill behind three military trucks on their way north. The sky is filling with fat, gray storm clouds. We continue into the mountains past neat rows of banana trees. On the outskirts of Esteli is a beautiful new school. Near it, a sewer trunk line is being installed.

Common sights along the road: people riding horse-back, usually 2 to a mount; adobe houses with red tile roofs; new schools in almost every community; cows, often in the road as well as next to it; spick and span new buildings of co-op farms, one with a cement basketball court next to it.

Ocotal

It is late afternoon. Now we are getting into rugged mountains. At first, there are massive trees, rocky cliffs, and a pale green river curving far below. Higher yet are the strange spiky pineapple fields and always the wildly orange Poinciana trees. Fields of dark earth lie freshly turned and ready for planting when the rains come to stay. Then soon the mountains are bald, only an occasional pine tree giving evidence of what was.

In a moment, we are over the bridge that has been blown up three times and into the mountain town of Ocotal. Our hotel turns out to be a cross between a motel and a pioneer fortress. The bus pulls through a 10-foot high gate set in a spiked iron fence, and into a compound of Hemingway-esque seedy elegance – complete with a murky swimming pool. Under bamboo cabanas men sit at knotty pine tables drinking beer from a forest of bottles.

Marilyn and I share a room. It is pleasant and spacious with the piney look of a mountain resort. One be must constantly reminding oneself that instead of skiers or hikers, though, the hills out there are crawling with murderous Contras.

The stockade nature of the lodgings makes me feel pretty safe until I open the back door of the room. It leads out to a balcony one story above the street. It would be no problem for any reasonably fit Contra to climb up here tonight and slit our throats. For now, however, the balcony is a great vantage point from which to take pictures of the town; red tiled roofs amid lavish green trees, children, chickens, and a big momma pig with her two babies.

An old man passing by in the dusty street below, smiles up at me as I take a picture of the pigs.

"*Hola*!" I call down to him.

"*Que tal?*" He asks with a friendly wave.

It is lovely to perch here on the railing and watch village life go by. Lovely, at least as long as I forget that the Honduran border is just at the edge of town.

There is a knock at the door. Debby says it is time to leave for our appointment at the church so we go back into the courtyard and prepare to board the bus. Here inside the stockade all is gaiety. A radio plays loud Latin tunes and empty beer bottles fill up the tabletops.

But outside there is tension. Soldiers patrol the street. One-story adobe buildings stand shoulder to shoulder along the rutted roads and bear their bullet scars in uneasy silence. Here war belongs not to the past, but the present. Sandino, in painted silhouette, braces himself against a wall and seems about to slip inside for cover.

Just as we alight from the bus at the church, the sky opens up on us and on the children playing basketball in the court outside. We all rush for the missionaries' house and in a few moments, the playground is a brown river.

In the small living room, three Nicaraguan ladies have displayed embroidered shirts and seed necklaces that they have made. We make some purchases and then seat ourselves on the sofa and on folding chairs. Our missionary hostess begins to talk:

"Our work here is with the C.D. groups. These are block groups and they are to defend ourselves. Ocotal has been attacked many times. Day before yesterday there was an alert and we had to stay up all night. The other night I thought the Contra were right in town because the mortars were so loud. It is a terrible sound, louder than anything we heard during the Revolution.

"There's one good thing, though. The Contra don't have to take their weapons with them when they run back to the border because the U.S. gives them all the weapons they want free. So they leave everything behind and our militia is capturing some sophisticated weaponry to defend us with. The propaganda of the Contras calls the Sandinistas 'atheistic' and 'Communist," but they are not. A few individual Sandinistas may be atheists or Communists, but there are some individuals like that in the U.S., too."

The Nicaraguan women who came to sell their crafts stand quietly in the background as we talk. They look very tired and sad. There is no gaiety here. Now that it is raining, we will be trapped here if the bridge is blown up again tonight. When the river rises, there is no other way out.

The oldest of the Nicaraguan ladies tells her story: "We live in grief and mourning. There is always so much death and destruction around us. The Contra come all the way up to my house on the edge of town. Three people were killed near here today.

"One night about 600 Contras came up to the edge of our house. They painted 'Christ yesterday, Christ today, and Christ always; death to Tomas Borge [one of the founders of the Sandinista Movement] and all the other thieves' on our house."

The lady pulls some photographs of her house out of her skirt pocket and we pass them around. The graffiti is as she has described it, in ugly black spray paint. I wonder how Christ would feel about having his name used in such a way.

Our missionary hostess begins to speak again, "One night recently the Contras moved in at 9:00 or 10:00 p.m. and attacked at 2:00 a.m. Five people from the town were killed. At about 8:00 a.m., they left again and headed toward the mountains."

Question: "Do foreign airplanes fly over here often?"

"There are some. One night a CDS patrolman saw a strange light in the sky with no noise. About a week later, we found out they'd been sending balloons over. Marguerite, who had joined our group in Managua after a month of duty as a Witness for Peace says, "When I was in Jalapa there were spy balloons coming over all the time."

The missionary continues, "When the tracer bullets go over it's just like fireworks. It would be beautiful if they didn't bring death."

The Nicaraguan woman begins again, "You hear one thing..."

Suddenly the lights flicker and go out. My stomach leaps into my chest. We are sitting in twilight dimness, but the lady goes on. I guess she's used to this.

"...one thing on the radio from Honduras, but it is not the reality of what happens here in Nicaragua. It is the Contra propaganda."

Another of the Nicaraguan women, a lovely girl about 16 years old says, "The Contras kidnapped my father and my 3 brothers and took them to Honduras. They told them there are Communists here and that they should fight. They are probably afraid to come back because if they do the Contra will think of a reprisal to use against us. I know one family who went to Honduras. They tried to come back under the amnesty, but the Contra set up ambushes to kill them."

As the lights come back on, the missionary says, "In one block of Mozente [not sure I spelled that right] 150 people; men, women, and children, were kidnapped. Ninety-three of them managed to come back and the woman gave birth on the road."

"What do the Contra do with people when they kidnap them?"

The girl answers, "sometimes they take them away and kill them. They pulled out my friend's eyes and fingernails. We found his body in the valley by Jalapa called 'The Grapes'. They made one woman watch while they pulled out her husband's tongue and eyes and then did the same to all 7 of her children."

The third woman, who has not spoken before says, "The reason we left Jalapa is that they came to my house and took my husband and me out and said they were going to drink our blood if we did not leave with them. There were about 40 of them. They didn't take us that time, but they said they would be back so we just left our house and everything in it and came here."

Question: "Have the Sandinistas ever done things like this to you? Have you heard of them doing such things to anyone?"

"No," the young girl answers, "the Contra try to tell people that the Sandinistas do those things, but they have not. The Sandinistas are careful never to go into

Honduras though the Contra always try to provoke them to."

We take our leave with thanks and handshakes all around. We'll be back later, but now it is time to go get some dinner. Darkness falls damply as water flows through the dirt streets and over my toes. The air is quite cool. My voice, which has grown hoarse, works as sporadically as the electricity (which is off again.)

We follow Mike through a doorway in one of the blank adobe facades, and find ourselves in a vast, empty, pitch dark space. The only light is a tiny pinpoint of candle flickering behind a window in another room. That's something I didn't think of about war —nothing works; no lights, no radio, no TV. There is just this feeling of befuddlement. An alarm begins to sound outside but we have no idea what it is or what we are supposed to do about it so we just pretend not to hear it.

We fumble our way to three card tables arranged against a wall. They seem to be the only furniture in this space. Kay, Mary Catherine, Marilyn, and I sit together at one card table and do our best to make cheerful conversation.

Later

We seem to have been sitting in the dark for quite a long time. There are children in here somewhere. I can hear, but not see, them. I've begun to write by the light of the small flashlight I keep in my purse. A couple of the group members at another table are arguing about whether or not we should tell of the atrocities when we get home. Will anyone believe us or will they simply tune out our whole message? It's the same argument as the other night in Managua, only here everyone is on edge and one of the girls has started to cry....

At this point, I had to stop writing because Sister Mary had to use my flashlight to find the bathroom. While she was gone our dinners came, but we had no idea of what they consisted. We poked at whatever was on the plates. Was it salad, which we know we aren't supposed to eat because it might make us sick? And what on earth was that flashing and crashing outside? The deep, reverberating booms that I felt as much as heard, were like no thundershower I've ever experienced. So, here we are, three middle-aged ladies possibly about to die in a bombardment and we're actually discussing whether or not to eat salad because we might get sick?

Still Later

Now we are back at the missionary house. The lights are on and our feet are getting dry. The message isn't any more cheerful, though. One horror follows another as the missionary tells us:

"The Contra commonly begin with the fingers and cut off the arms a small piece at a time...

In an adjoining room, a group of women have gathered to say the Rosary. Their voices bleed through the wall like the background of a dream.

"...in September the town of Santa Maria was shelled from 6:15 a.m. to 5:00 p.m. It was a terrible, terrible experience for those people. Sometimes they just pull you into the house and talk and talk. The strategy of the Contra in our area is just to keep the people on edge because there's nothing much for them to destroy, no coffee farms – the only possible objective is terrorism. Things are hard here, but to see the people's strength, joy, and unselfishness is amazing.

"You know none of the people are trained for what they are doing. One of the Junta members is quoted as saying, 'After the Revolution we thought we could change things in a day, then after a year we thought it might take a few years, now we think maybe two generations.' When Daniel Ortega was asked 'What have you learned since you became chief of the Junta?' he said, 'everything.'

"You have to remember that our situation here in the North is difficult because that is where Somoza recruited most of his National Guard. After the Revolution most of them went to Honduras, but their families are still here, so when they come back their families protect them out of family loyalty."

Question: "Do you, as a religious worker, feel repressed by the government?"

"No, I don't. In Mexico the last person you would turn to for help is a soldier or policeman. Here they are so courteous and friendly. I have never seen any sign of mistreatment of anyone by a soldier."

Question: "Have any churches had to close? Is there repression?"

"No church has been closed. What few problems there were have been in Managua. There was one priest there who incited the students to take over a school.

They killed some Sandinista soldiers and then he was expelled from the country.

"How has the church responded to the revolution in this area?"

"Remember that Somoza would not allow any political parties or opposition so the church became the main place where things could be discussed. It still is. Everyone in our area is very supportive of the revolution because it has so many Christian values. But as the upper classes distance themselves from the revolution, the Hierarchy goes with them. It confuses the people. They have been taught to respect their bishops.

"After Vatican II the laity was given a stronger role and so it is a real crisis for priests as to what is their real role and authority."

"Do you know of any Cuban soldiers in your area?"

"Not soldiers, there were doctors. At most we had 9 Cuban doctors but a few months ago, very quietly, most of them left. The Cuban doctors are all very fine and very dedicated. They are forbidden to talk politics and so are the teachers. They must respect the customs of our people. If they don't respect these rules, they are sent home. Actually some of the Cubans have been converted to Christianity here so the influence is actually in the OTHER direction."

"What do the soldiers do for food when there is a battle that goes on for a long time?"

"They just don't eat. The worst is thirst, they tell me. They say that sometimes they are so thirsty they just want to bite a tree."

Marilyn says, "A Sandinista soldier told me that the Contras are very demoralized and need high pay and other incentives because they have nothing else to fight for. He also believes that their food is drugged to enable them to carry out such dreadful crimes, but no one knows for sure."

The missionary continues: "You know, though, Nicaragua is not Grenada. It will not be so easy to conquer even if there is an invasion by the U.S. One woman said to me, 'my husband and two sons are at the border defending us. I lost two sons in the Revolution. If all the men are killed we women will take up arms and defend our country.'

"We know things are not perfect here. We have many problems. When we went to talk with Daniel Ortega he was very shy at first, then he said, 'Can you give me any suggestions? What are some of the things we've done wrong?' To me the humility he showed was wonderful. Can you imagine President Reagan speaking like that? I once taught Social Studies in the U.S. and now I am horrified at what we've done, taught to trust in our government so unquestioningly, so now you see the results. People in the U.S. don't question what their government does."

The older Nicaraguan lady is back by herself tonight. She begins to tell us about her work as director of the day care center.

"So far we have 180 children from 45 days old to 6 years. It's the first time there has ever been such a service in Ocotal. None of us at the center has any such experience, but we are getting used to it. We are learning.

"The financing for our center came from Canada and we've been open for three months now. Before we opened, the children were locked in their houses alone all day while the mothers worked. We prepare special food for the babies and for the children who are malnourished. We also have a mother's milk bank."

The missionary speaks again: "Nicaragua now has the lowest cost of living of any Central American country. Not everyone is happy with the new government though. One lady was complaining to me that she has to pay taxes on her eight houses. She is a professional landlord and her complaint against the Revolution is that she must pay taxes and respect a profit ceiling."

There are sharp reports from a rifle somewhere outside. The lady who had been telling us about the preschool asks to be excused and leaves in a hurry. The missionary continues:

"In our women's group we are trying to overcome selfishness so we work as a group. Four of us went out to gather seeds for the necklaces. We have charts and the women keep track of how many hours they work. At first some thought they could just sit back and let others do everything, but we showed how it is better to work together because we can buy materials together and we can share things like sewing machines and paints.

From where I sit near the open door, I see two soldiers run through the wet basketball court. They are illuminated for a moment by the light from the windows.

"You know some workers here have learned to make their own parts for sewing machines. Our people are becoming very creative in dealing with shortages."

A uniformed man appears at the door and knocks. He is the government official who we had been told was coming to talk with us. He is very young, in his early twenties perhaps, but as always with these young people, I am struck by his gentle dignity. He smiles easily but as he begins to explain why he is late, he struggles with emotion. Two of his *companeros* have just been killed.

He tells us that six thousand Contras have infiltrated between here and Matagalpa. They are being resupplied by airdrops flying over Nicaragua from Honduran bases. The young man says, "We have been able to detect and destroy most of the groups of Contra, they are called 'Task Forces,' [an American term if ever I heard one!] but we have paid a high price in the deaths of our comrades. In this area now there are only about two hundred Contra left.

A poster falls off the wall and everyone jumps.

He continues without taking notice. "We are expecting enemy action soon near here. We are on a situation of alert and are ready to repel any attackers."

He shows us on a map where the main fighting is taking place. It is between here and Matagalpa. I hope Leticia is all right! He explains that the bulk of the Contra force is invading right now. Joint U.S. and Honduran "exercises" are finishing up just the other side of the hills that we see from our balcony. They will conclude next week.

"Right now," he says, his sagging into his chair with obvious exhaustion, "the Contras are trying to take over some territory and use it for a provisional government. We are trying to encircle them so that they can't return to Honduras. Most of these Contra are ex-National Guardsmen [Somoza's soldiers], but some are kidnapped peasants and foreign advisors. A Panamanian and a Puerto Rican were killed near here recently."

Question: "What happens to the Contras who surrender?"

"They are tried and if they are found guilty of crimes committed while Guardsmen before the Revolution, they are sentenced to prison. If their crimes are not great and they can be rehabilitated they are sent back to their families. Of those who have surrendered to us and those who have been killed, we have identified many former Guardsmen. They have been trying to cover up their past and present themselves as Christian crusaders. They are trying to give the impression also, that they are disgruntled peasants. Of course it's true that many were peasants before they were National Guardsmen!"

Question: "Where are the 20,000 Cuban troops that Reagan says are stationed in Nicaragua?"

The young man looks flabbergasted at first, then laughs, shaking his head. "They're in the hospitals working and in the schools teaching. If there really were 20,000 we wouldn't have any health problems!"

Outside the night has become very quiet: a wet, heavy quiet.

Question: "Has anyone abused Contra prisoners?"

"I know of no cases in this sector. We do not wish to do to them what they did to us."

This boy is so young and so exhausted. Even when speaking the unspeakable he shows no anger, only sadness. He is about the age of my own sons. I want to shout at someone, "Leave him alone!" I want to go out and shout those words into the ugly, wet darkness closing in around us.

Question: "Do you think the bridge will be destroyed again soon? Is there a plan to evacuate the city if it is?"

"Between here and the border is a line of military defense. Here in the city we have a second line of defense in the citizens. In the case of a longer war, Ocotal would be very difficult to evacuate. The closest place to go is Esteli, which is an hour away by truck. We have bomb shelters here and we will try to protect the children and the old people."

Kay asks, "Have the Witnesses for Peace helped and would more of them be useful?"

"Yes, we have seen effects of that program. It helps the world to know that Nicaragua wants peace and it helps Nicaragua to know that it is not the people of the U.S. that want war. The Contras know that the Witness for Peace are there and if they attacked they would show the criminality of the Contras to the world, but if there were a large attack they would not respect your nationality. Internationals have already been killed though we do all we can to protect them."

Question: "Are the Contras doing this terrorism because they don't know any better or is it a deliberate terrorism campaign?"

"It is part of a military strategy that the National Guard had before the Revolution and that they still continue. The purpose is to frighten the population into not cooperating with the Sandinista government."

He looks at his watch and stands to leave. "And now I must get back," he says, "I want to thank you all for coming to see us. If we could show you more of the truth, we would be glad to. The cost of this revolution is very great, but we believe it to be worth it."

As our bus wallows back to the motel we pass through streets that are dark and, except for armed sentries, deserted. The bus passes through the stockade gate and Bill and I joke about "Fort Apache." The hotel itself is even called, *"Frontier,"* meaning "border" in English.

Inside the compound is such a special and intense little world that I sit by the murky swimming pool for a long time even though I know I should get some sleep. If we have an attack tonight it'll probably roust us out at an awful hour!

Chapter Thirteen

Mothers' Day in Ocotal

Sunday Morning

No major artillery attack last night. We were lucky. Some strange things were going on, though, that involved a lot of shouting and pounding. I got up finally when my curiosity could take it no longer, and looked out the back door into the dark street below. A group of men were outside the house behind us, shouting and pounding on its front door. I remembered the lady's story about the Contra writing on her house and wondered if this was more of the same. I was too sleepy to stand there very long, though, so I just locked the door and went to bed. The noise went on for a long time but I decided that if someone wanted to chop me in small pieces they'd have to wake me up to do it.

This morning I am perched on the balcony railing again. The little house across the street is still intact and unsullied, so I guess the incident last night was not important. All is tranquility now. Occasionally the sun breaks through the clouds, which cling to the hillsides and dip into the valleys. Boys play marbles in the street and roosters crow as if they were trying to get a whole week's worth of work over in one day.

A military truck approaches slowly down the street, which is already dusty again even after last night's rain, and the pedestrians move aside. It passes and the foot traffic resumes; women dressed for church, men pulling carts filled with bundles, chickens pecking in the mud of a narrow ravine.

This morning we have been given a choice of activities. We can either go to Mass at the church on the Plaza, or we can accompany a nun to her Bible study class for women. I am anxious to do the latter, but I discover that only Marilyn; Mike's wife, Becky, and I are going with the nun. As we jolt up the rutted roads toward the hills, I feel the anxiety beginning - four religious workers in a jeep! Remember the nuns in El Salvador! The most eventful part of the trip, however, is when the sister and I have to get out of the jeep to move a large, dead cactus that is blocking the road. There was a moment, however, when the thought passed through my mind that this could be a Contra trap – possibly complete with land mine. I shrugged it off. *Que sera sera.*

The school where the women's group is to meet is on an exposed knoll outside of town. A new school is being constructed right next to it. When Marilyn and the sister decide to go back to town for Marilyn's concertina, leaving Rita and me here alone with 9 little girls, I remember that new schools are a favorite Contra target. Oddly enough, I am able to control my panic far better than I could at the L.A. airport. I wonder why. I just know that I am not going to let anyone hurt these kids and that determination alone gives me strength.

On the way out here, the sister told us that today's group meeting would be different than the usual Sunday morning class because the Nicaraguan Mother's Day was only 3 days away. The girls had decided to take charge of preparations in order to honor their mothers.

So now, the girls, ranging in age from about fourteen to five, are busy putting up homemade posters and fastening plastic flowers to the wall with scotch tape. One of the older girls writes the word, "Agenda," on the board and neatly prints the morning's schedule under it. A boy outside cups his hands and looks in the window wondering, perhaps, what these women are planning.

I sit in a battered classroom chair and, as I watch the girls write on the board, I think how familiar and comfortable is the setting. The sound of chalk on a blackboard is one that I've heard as background music over all my years as a teacher. The smell of the room, the sounds of children are all so frighteningly normal. For the first time in my life, I suddenly understand that this is the horror of war - that it takes place in normal settings and kills real people. War does not happen in some Technicolor fourth dimension, some far-off battlefield, but in someone's backyard, farmyard, school yard.

One of the homemade posters on the wall consists of a large sheet of construction paper with the words, "Our Community," written in crayon at the top and photographs pasted on it. There are several pictures of a party the children gave for the old people, of a Christmas pageant with the usual bath-robed shepherds, and in one corner is the picture of the casket of a boy killed by the Contra. Death, cruel and unnatural, is a part of community life in Ocotal.

Now, I realize, is the perfect time to get the children's drawings I had hoped to take home with me, but all of my carefully collected materials are back at the motel! I hadn't realized there would be children here. As Marilyn and the sister return, I am tearing pages from my notebook and passing them out. Sister has some crayons and soon everyone is working hard on messages for the North Americans. Boys have joined us now, too. I am amazed at the politeness of the children. Not only do they wait their turns for paper, but when I hand them some they voluntarily pass it on to the next child. Such great care is taken with the crayons! Each one is carefully replaced in the box after use.

And now the room is filling up. The mothers have arrived. The girls have made beautiful construction paper nametags for all of us with flowers and butterflies stenciled on in crayon. There are about forty women and children in the room. We begin to sing to the accompaniment of Marilyn's concertina and Sister's ukulele.

After several songs we move to the next item on the agenda; the welcome, which is delivered by an earnest junior high age girl. Next comes the Bible study lesson during which Sister asks, "Who was first at the Tomb and discovered that Jesus was gone?"

"The women," is the quick reply.

There follows a lively discussion about the many things that women can do and the role of women in the home and community. As the lesson proceeds, rifle shots are heard occasionally. They are loud and close. Everyone looks nervously out the window, but Sister pretends not to have heard.

After the lesson, a pretty girl of 12 or 14 in an immaculate pink dress, stands to deliver a report that she has written out on tablet paper in a neat, rounded, schoolgirl script.

When she finishes, she explains that the pictures on our nametags are intended to be a way of assigning us to our small groups. My group, those with roses on their nametags, consists of six people; a quietly handsome teenaged boy, two women about my own age, and one lady wizened and bent with age. I am embarrassed because everyone is so neat and clean and nicely dressed and I am still wearing the same jeans I've been living in for the past two days.

The girl in pink rushes from group to group, notebook in hand, a pencil gripped between her teeth, making sure that everyone understands the assignment. We are discussing the Virgin of Guadalupe, but I don't quite catch the details (in Spanish, of course!) It concerns something about motherhood and the fact that the Virgin appeared to a poor Indian man.

Even though I don't understand everything that is going on, it is wonderful to see these peasant women, who before the Revolution would have been condemned to a lifetime of illiteracy, discussing their own ideas with confidence then writing carefully in their notebooks. I am reminded of the expression on Fernando Cardinal's face as he told about the letters that the newly literate peasants had sent to him. To see minds opening like flowers in the sun is indeed a religious experience.

Later

It is now nearly noon. The meeting has been going on since about 9:30. My Spanish is entirely gone, worn out along with the rest of me. My throat is very sore. In spite of my linguistic limitations, the women have been very accepting of me. They seem anxious to know about women in the U.S. so I explain to them about the work of our women's group in Los Angeles and how we have united to fight the deportation of Salvadorans. They seem favorably impressed.

One of the women, who is about my age, points to my wedding ring and smiles. The older one looks at my (modest size) diamond and nods curtly as if to say, "You see, she is rich."

The girl in pink comes to hear our group report. We dictate and she writes with a felt tipped pen on a long sheet of newsprint. As she finishes, she reads the report back to us and the group members make changes and corrections. As we move our chairs back into one large group, I listen to the women's neighborhood small talk. My Spanish is still functioning well enough to understand that it is all about death.

Our group is first to report. All of us go to the front along with our large piece of newsprint. When we finish, we are applauded, as is each group in their turn.

After the singing of more songs, Sister begins to read letters from church people in the U.S., which Debby gave to her last night to share with the ladies here today. Even as Sister reads aloud the words of friendship and support, shots are heard again. The women sitting nearest the windows look anxiously outside.

But the words of human understanding are stronger than fear and, one by one, the faces turn away from the windows and back to Sister ("...your sufferings are our sufferings...") with streaming eyes. For them to know that all of the people in that immense and powerful country to the north do not hate them or desire their deaths is apparently a tremendously moving experience for them.

One letter says, "I think we are crucifying Jesus every time a Nicaraguan child dies of hunger or a Contra bullet."

Now it is time for the children to recite the pieces they have prepared in honor of their mothers. One tiny girl, about 5 years old, has memorized a poem. She recites it flawlessly with hand gestures and vivid expression. Two older girls, perhaps 10 or 12, sing two songs in carefully practiced harmony.

As he watches this entertainment, a boy of 9 or 10 chews absentmindedly on a straight pin from someone's nametag. My years as a teacher and as a mother impel me to warn him..."be careful! Don't hurt yourself!"

But my words die unspoken. My concern, when he is close enough for me to touch, is instinctive. Yet, what about the *real* concern that is needed? What good would it do to save him from the dangers of a straight pin if I have already purchased, through my tax money, the Contra bullet or artillery shell that will kill him?

Chapter Fourteen

Home Again

We returned to Managua in a downpour. Our bus leaked but we were all too tired to care. Two days later, we returned to our safe, comfortable homes in the U.S.

Now, a few days after that, Dave and I are sitting under umbrellas in the honey-sweet California sunshine on the patio of our favorite cafe. The sounds of suburban conversation and the happy clatter of coffee cups adds a melody of well being to the Symphony of Home. Everything is as it should be: brick-fronted shops, matrons in tennis outfits, and sparrows picking up crumbs.

But Dave sets down his coffee cup and hands me the section of morning paper, which he has been reading. It is folded back to an inner page.

"I hate to show you this...," he began, "...but there was a massive Contra attack in Ocotal. Isn't that the place you were telling me about?"

I took the paper. The item was very small, only a paragraph. *"A thousand Contra... early morning hours... heavy casualties..."*

As I read the scanty facts, I am seeing again the faces of the women listening to Sister read the letters. Their tears had been tears of hope. It was with hope they had said good bye to me, hope that by telling their story I could prevent more nights of terror – that I could prevent the very thing that happened only days later.

In their letters to us in the U.S., the children had written, over and over, *"We hope that more of you will come to visit us. We hope that your government will give us peace."* One of the older girls had written, *"I pray that there may not be war in Nicaragua. That those invaders who come to kill children and poor people may not come."*

I must admit that I went to Nicaragua with a bias. I expected to find enemies. In a sense I needed to find enemies so that I could say, "Of course my government is right!" Then I would be spared the pain of concerning myself with such a difficult and terrible subject as war in a far away land.

How nice it would have been to be able to leave it to the experts! But I heard the experts on Maundy Thursday at the restaurant on the hill and what they offer is depersonalized death – *"Saturate the field."* They did it in Ocotal.

So now, I talk to everyone who will listen, telling my story like the sailor with the albatross, not because I want to, but because I must.

The last entry in my journal was written on the way to the airport, as we were about to leave Nicaragua. In it I wrote:

"I see everywhere, in vacant lots, in median strips on the boulevards, in the spaces between the little wood and metal houses, the hopeful green shoots of grass revived by the first rains of the year. You cannot kill the grass; its will to live eventually triumphs over every work of man. In the same way, the people of Latin America will eventually control their own destinies. No matter what new cruelties we inflict on them, the day will come when they can lay down their burdens, stand up straight, look the world in the eye, and smile."

AFTERWORD

It is hot in California. In the south, over the freeway, the sky is pale as pavement. Even the dogs prefer to stay inside by the air conditioner. They lie panting on the cool kitchen floor.

Our children are visiting, Randy from San Diego and Rob, Patty and the baby from Phoenix. We are all having fun with the baby and playing marathon games of Trivial Pursuit when the mailman drops a letter from Nicaragua through the slot. It is from Sister Mary.

Dear Rachael,

Did you remember that I was running to catch the bus to Ocotal the last time I saw you? Yes, believe it or not, I was IN Ocotal during the attack. Rifle fire and machine gun shots blasted through the dawn's darkness and woke us up. The Contras had crossed over the border and were attacking the town.

We three sisters and one catechist huddled in the small hallway of our house under a table with a mattress pulled on top from 4:30 am to 7:30 am and again from 8:30 am to 10:30 am. During that time, we heard about fifty explosions and continuous gunfire. Bullets smashed into the roof of our house, which, you remember, is connected to the church. Rachael, I really felt I was going to die. I began praying

"Jesus my Confidence" and placed my life in God's hands.

We could hear sounds of shouting and explosions coming nearer the house. We were cramped and sweating from heat and fear. Every now and then, the impact caused some plaster to fall from the ceiling. Finally, when it seemed that the shouting and explosions were more in the distance we went out to see what we could do.

We spent the day visiting those who were recovering their dead, trying to comfort and be with them in some small way. What is so hard for us is to know that our government is financing all this. In the still smoking rubble of the coffee plant, the lumberyard, the granary, we found bullet jackets from U.S. weapons and cardboard shell cases with NATO written on them. As we stood in front of the charred and still burning beans and corn from the silos it was impossible for us to imagine how anyone could think they were achieving anything by burning the food supplies. These people have worked so very hard in their fields for the so very little they have..."Fruit of the vine - the sweat, the toil - the work of human hands."

At the cemetery the next day, our ears were filled with the sobs and cries of family members who were burying their loved ones. We went from grave to grave, from family to family to hug and pray and console...the fact that we are North Americans elicited no rejection from them. They understand how much people in the U.S feel and vigil with them. Let us pray for each other...